THE
POPE
IS
Not
GAY!

The Pope Is Not Gay!

by

Angelo Quattrocchi

Translation by Romy Clark Giuliani

VERSO

London • New York

This edition first published by Verso 2010
© Verso 2010
Translation Romy Clark Giuliani © 2010
First published as *No, No, No! Ratzy non è gay!*
© malatempora editrice 2007

Every effort has been made to trace copyright holders and to
obtain their permission for the use of copyright material. The
publisher apologises for any errors or omissions and would be
grateful if notified of any corrections that should be incorporated
in future reprints or editions of this book.

1 3 5 7 9 10 8 6 4 2

Verso
UK: 6 Meard Street, London W1F 0EG
US: 20 Jay Street, Suite 1010, Brooklyn, NY 11201
www.versobooks.com

Verso is the imprint of New Left Books

ISBN-13: 978-1-84467-474-9

British Library Cataloguing in Publication Data
A catalogue record for this book is available from the British Library

Library of Congress Cataloging-in-Publication Data
A catalog record for this book is available from the Library of Congress

Typeset in Minion by Hewer Text UK Ltd, Edinburgh

Printed and bound in the UK by Scotprint, Haddington, Scotland

Contents

Appendices: The Vatican's Position on Homosexuality as Detailed by the Congregation for the Doctrine of the Faith

Contents

1

It's a Long Story:
From St Paul to Pope Benedict XVI

29 June 1951: the feast of saints Peter and Paul. A perfect summer's day in Freising, and Cardinal Michael Faulhaber, a good man who was one of the first prominent figures to oppose Hitler, is ordaining around forty priests in the city's beautiful cathedral. Among them are the brothers Georg and Joseph Ratzinger. The young Joseph is twenty-three, three years younger than his robust brother, and he takes it all in with eyes that are bright, lively, and cunning. When Joseph kneels in front of the old cardinal (and the story is Ratzinger's, taken from his auto-hagiography), he is blessed with a sign:

> We should not be superstitious [note that 'should not be']; but, at the moment when the elderly bishop laid his hands on me, a little bird – perhaps a lark – flew up from the high altar in the cathedral

and trilled a little joyful song. And I could not but see in this a reassurance from on high, as if I heard the words 'This is good, you are on the right path.'[1]

True, it's not quite on a par with the little shepherd girls' vision of the Madonna or Joan of Arc seeing Saint Margaret and Saint Genevieve at a critical moment in French history, but it's still a sign straight out of Hollywood, a depiction of religious life in Bavaria anyone could grasp. And the lark – who sings hymns at Heaven's gate – is a highly appropriate sign for the man who would later become the Holy Inquisitor and then pope Benedict XVI (nicknamed 'Ratzy' in Italy), scourge of homosexuals and all non-reproductive sexual practices.

The long history of sex-phobia in the Holy Roman Church did not begin with our papal hero. It took root in the early centuries of Western Christianity with St Paul, of whom Andrew Priest, psychologist, anthropologist and protestant priest, has this to say:

> He found sex disgusting and he was profoundly hostile to it. He suffered from a pathological lack of

---

1   Joseph Ratzinger, *Milestones: Memoirs 1927–1977*, translated by E. Leiva- Merikakis, Ignatius 1988, p. 99. [The translations of quotations, unless otherwise indicated, are mine – RCG].

emotional maturity and was psychologically unstable, and was therefore too apt to confuse his instinctive reactions and capricious value judgments with rules emanating from on high ... He did not appear to have properly understood Jesus' message. He was more attracted to Christ on the cross than he was to the Christ of the resurrection. His doctrine of atonement bears the mark of his sadomasochistic tastes ...

At the beginning of his career, his violent persecution of Christians betrays a strong sadistic tendency, and when he talks about his suffering, especially his self-flagellation, from which he seems to have derived some kind of pleasure, his masochistic tendencies are obvious. There is also good reason to think that he was a repressed homosexual and that deep down he rationalized his sexual orientation by turning to chastity ...

There is good cause to believe that he was unmarried and that as a consequence ardent Jews viewed him with suspicion. There is no doubt that he persecuted the Christians with such violence in order to make amends for this perceived flaw. And later, when he converted to Christianity, he justified his unmarried status by inventing the doctrine of chastity.[2]

---

2   Andrew Priest, 'Un homosexual peut-il être Chrétien?' ['Can a Homosexual Be a Christian?'], *Arcadie*, no. 160 (April 1967).

Here, of course, we are talking about Saint Paul, not Ratzinger. As far as we know, Ratzy was only once – and then hesitantly – asked about his 'adolescent relationships', experiences that make no appearance in his preening memoirs. And our hero – of the tight smile and the satirical, sparkling eyes – replied that the book of his life was just an outline … and there let the matter rest. In short, he skated over the issue with characteristic composure, leaving himself free to return to his chosen task of castigating the world in the course of imposing Church doctrine.

Yet it would be enlightening, from a psychological standpoint, to know whether he became inhibited at such an early age that the normal masturbatory tendencies of young men were staunched in him during adolescence. This is very relevant to our inquiry, because as psychology suggests, the repression he suffered in those dark, wretched days in Nazi Germany brought about his sad condemnation of all sexual practices not approved by canon law. But his relationships with both men and women are doomed to remain buried in the sacristies of Bavaria.

One thing is certain. Sex became an obsession with him. Why this occurred is intriguing. Concerning two

key moments of his adolescence – his two years as a young soldier of the Reich, and his experience with homo- and heterosexuality – we have, respectively, only an official account and absolutely nothing. Nobody has wanted to make too much of his enforced membership of the Reich, and this is understandable. But it is clear that his adolescent sexual experiences must have influenced his adult life and thus prepared the way for his zealous homophobia and his insistence on chastity for homosexuals; for his total refusal to allow priests to marry (though lately a special dispensation has been offered for disaffected Anglican ministers who convert to Roman Catholicism). And again, it explains his persistent, dogmatic defence of the sacred indissoluble ties of marriage and of the family, to the exclusion of any other design for living – a paradigm which is truly out of date.

Ratzy is fighting a losing rearguard battle in a world dominated by market forces that are driving us away from the nuclear family, encouraging us to live on our own as singletons with more or less mercenary dealings with both sex and sentiment. And faced with the gradual collapse of the nuclear family, this man, who is certainly not stupid, has since becoming Pope taken up arms against a sea of public indifference to set himself up as the improbable champion of the 'till death do us part' obligations of the sacred union. His backward vision makes marriage an indestructible fortress, and, in Italy, the grotesque consequences of this can be witnessed every day by anyone with access to a television.

On 29 December 1975, Franjo Seper, our hero's predecessor in the Sant'Uffizio, the Office of the Holy Roman Inquisition – now rebranded for modern sensibilities as the Congregation for the Doctrine of the Faith – issues a document entitled *Declaration On Certain Questions Concerning Sexual Ethics*. It brings with it a tiny ray of hope after two thousand years spent condemning sodomites. Below I quote in full the section of the *Declaration* dealing with homosexuality. It is a masterpiece of Jesuit reasoning, both oozing with embarrassment at increasingly liberal attitudes and behaviour and at the same time concerned to keep the bastions of doctrine intact, while throwing the tiniest of bones to a more permissive age:

> At the present time there are those who, basing themselves on observations in the psychological order, have begun to judge indulgently, and even to excuse completely, homosexual relations between certain people. This they do in opposition to the constant teaching of the Magisterium and to the moral sense of the Christian people.

A distinction is drawn, and it seems with some reason, between homosexuals whose tendency comes from a false education, from a lack of normal sexual development, from habit, from bad example, or from other similar causes, and is transitory or at least not incurable; and homosexuals who are definitely such because of some innate instinct or a pathological constitution judged to be incurable. In regard to this second category of subjects, some people conclude that their tendency is so natural that it justifies in their case homosexual relations within a sincere communion of life and love analogous to marriage, in so far as such homosexuals feel incapable of enduring a solitary life.

In the pastoral field, these homosexuals must certainly be treated with understanding and sustained in the hope of overcoming their personal difficulties and their inability to fit into society. Their culpability will be judged with prudence. But no pastoral method can be employed which would give moral justification to these acts on the grounds that they should be consonant with the condition of such people. For according to the objective moral order [!], homosexual relations are acts which lack an essential and indispensable finality. In Sacred Scripture they are condemned as a serious depravity and even presented as the sad consequence of rejecting God. [The explanation for this leap in logic can be found elsewhere.] This judgement of Scripture does not of course permit us to conclude that all those who suffer from this anomaly are personally responsible for it, but it does attest to the fact that homosexual acts are intrinsically disordered and can in no case be approved of. *The end.*

[Authorized Vatican translation, Section VIII]

The ultra-keen eye can detect a few hairline cracks in the rhetorical structure that allow a sliver of light into the obscurantist gloom which, for centuries, has led to people being discriminated against, ghettoized, burnt at the stake and assassinated. One has to look extremely carefully to discern the glimmer in the darkness. It's there, but it won't last long: ten years. A blink of an eye for a church that is many centuries old. Nonetheless they are long, liberating years for the movements stirring outside the granite walls of the Vatican: women discovered feminism and women's rights in the seventies; gays found their identity on that legendary night at Stonewall in the Village in New York, when they at last fought back for the first time against the umpteenth beating by the NYPD. And from then on there was no stopping them. They expressed and claimed their rights in the heart of the Big Apple and all over the world. Even in papal Rome and, who knows, maybe even inside the notoriously homosexual Vatican, as Peyrefitte wrote some fifty years ago in his best-selling *The Keys of St. Peter*.[3]

In October 1986, our little hero, the inquisitor, arrives on the scene at the request of the jovial pope who wants to restore the old order,[4] and he quickly produces the *Letter to the Bishops of the Catholic Church on the Pastoral care of Homosexuals*.[5] His aim is to fill in the cracks before they get any bigger, to strengthen the walls of biblical and therefore eternal condemnation. It is the opening act of two decades of unrestrained homophobia. Listen to this:

> As in every moral disorder, homosexuality prevents one's own fulfilment and happiness by acting contrary to the creative wisdom of God. The Church, in rejecting erroneous opinions regarding homosexuality, does not limit but rather

---

3   [*Les Clés de Saint Pierre*] London: Secker & Warburg, 1957. Satirical novel about the inner workings of the Vatican, seized in the early 1950s by police in Italian bookshops on the grounds it abused religion.

4   John Paul II, the Polish Pope Wojtyla.

5   As Cardinal Ratzinger, Prefect of the Congregation for the Doctrine of the Faith.

defends personal freedom and dignity realistically and authentically understood.

[*Letter to the Bishops of the Catholic Church on the Pastoral Care of Homosexuals, 1986, p. 2. Official translation. See Appendix 1*]

Here you can experience our inquisitor's creed for yourself. I condemn you – he says – and as always I discriminate against you. But I do it to please my God and, of course, for your own good. Souls are good. Arseholes bad.

But those ten years did not pass in vain. The homosexual community roused itself and in a thousand courageous, witty, irreverent ways demonstrated its impatience with the two-thousand-year-old stigma imposed on them by the Church. And although the media treated these demonstrations as a bit of a freak show, the protests were effective.

Nonetheless, Ratzy continues along his path of subtle denigration, marginalization and repression. He uses the same methods employed in his other obscurantist battle, namely the fight to suppress liberation theology. Here is what he has to say about the growing gay movement:

One tactic used is to protest that any and all criticism of or reservations about homosexual people, their activity and lifestyle, are simply diverse forms of unjust discrimination [Ibid., p. 3].

This speaks for itself.
And again:

There is an effort in some countries to manipulate the Church by gaining the often well-intentioned support of her pastors with a view to changing civil-statutes and laws. This is done in order to conform to these pressure groups' concept that homosexuality is at least a completely harmless, if not an entirely good, thing. Even when the practice of homosexuality may seriously threaten the lives and well-being of a large number of people, its advocates remain undeterred and refuse to consider the magnitude of the risks involved.

And then, having said that 'the intrinsic dignity of each person must always be respected in word, in action and in law', he continues:

but the proper reaction to crimes committed against homosexual persons [Could he mean the Nazi massacres hushed up by the Church?] should not be to claim that the homosexual condition is not disordered. [This is the same refrain that his predecessor used.] When such a claim is made and when homosexual activity is consequently condoned, or when civil legislation is introduced to protect behaviour to which no-one has any conceivable right, neither the Church nor society at large should be surprised when other distorted notions and practices gain ground, and irrational and violent reactions increase.

But do you realize what the little inquisitor is saying in this hair-splitting, Jesuitical language?

And there's more:

'Sexual orientation' does not constitute a quality comparable to race, ethnic background, etc. in respect to non-discrimination. Unlike these, homosexual orientation is an objective disorder [*sic*] and evokes moral concern. There are areas in which it is not unjust discrimination to take sexual orientation into account, for example, in the placement of children for adoption or foster care, in employment of teachers or athletic coaches, and in military recruitment.[6]

---

6   This is actually taken from the 1992 document: 'Some Considerations Concerning the Response to Legislative Proposals on the Non-Discriminitation of Homosexual Persons', published by the Congregation of the Doctrine of the Faith [see Appendix 2].

In short, don't give your children to gays, give them to the parish priests (and if these turn out to be paedophiles, never fear, we'll take care of it).

Don't let gays into schools or the military! The word for this is marginalization. The obvious and inevitable response is: So much for Christian charity.

And finally:

> The 'sexual orientation' of a person is not comparable to race, sex, age, etc. also for another reason ... An individual's sexual orientation is generally not known to others unless he publicly identifies himself as having this orientation or unless some overt behaviour manifests it. As a rule, the majority of homosexually oriented persons who seek to lead chaste lives do not publicize their sexual orientation. Hence the problem of discrimination in terms of employment, housing, etc., does not usually arise.

The Letter to the Bishops on pastoral care was written when the gay rights movement was not as strong or widespread as now. Nevertheless, our hero orders gays to be chaste and hidden away. Unbelievable!

Then in 1992, on the subject of coming out, he writes:

Homosexual persons who assert their homosexuality tend to be precisely those who judge
homosexual behaviour or lifestyle to be 'either
completely harmless, if not an entirely good thing'
[*sic*] and hence worthy of public approval. It is from
this quarter that one is more likely to find those
who seek to 'manipulate the church by gaining the
often well-intentioned support of her pastors with a
view to changing civil statutes and laws.'

This is a masterpiece of duplicity, but also of far-
sightedness. Twenty years after the Letter, all the gay
pride festivals and the thousands of gays coming
out all over the Catholic and non-Catholic world,
from Rome to Sidney, have changed the game; they
have shifted the media power relations, if you like.
Advertising and marketing have discovered the
gay market and are not going to drop it now. The
monolithic, suffocating world of 'God, Country and
Family' has been torn to shreds and we now have a
world based on the rights of individuals to behave as
they see fit in the name of consumption. For good or
ill, it's definitely a very different place now and a long
way from Manichaean pontification.

And now, as Ratzinger feared, gays, those very
people who were demonized because of their
disorderly promiscuity, are asking to regularize their

relationships. You would expect some understanding on his part. After all, they are returning to the fold. On the contrary! Now that gays are starting to demand civil partnerships they have to be attacked even more strongly. Why? Because they undermine his idea of the sanctity of the family.

The long 1986 Letter that committed the whole of the Church to discriminate against and marginalize gays got the response it deserved from Franco Grillini, then secretary of the still fragile Arcigay association:[7]

> Any remaining space for dialogue between the Catholic Church and homosexuals has gone ... the Church has never issued such a humiliating invitation to discriminate against any other category: not against the mafia, not against the corrupt, not against those who rape ... the church is morally responsible for all acts of violence and discrimination against gays and lesbians that follow ...

The letter that sparked this anger is more than twenty years old, and the Vatican has done nothing

---

7   ARCI: *Associazione Ricreativa Culturale Italiana*, a broad left organization, which has a number of affiliated single-interest groups.

to diminish its offensiveness. Not a comma has been changed. In fact, since Ratzinger the Inquisitor is now Pope Benedict XVI, the reactionary negations of his letter now carry a papal endorsement.

So as not to bore you with all that turgid prose, bloated as it is with a rhetoric of nudges and winks, behind which hide entrenched positions, cruel solutions, stones thrown and the guilty hand quickly concealed, I list below, for the sake of clarity, all the 'nos' – the intransigent refusals – that our inquisitorial author includes in his long, suffocating text.

The first 'no' is to the chink of light left open by the humanity and decency of his predecessor after centuries of darkness, and which follows the deafening silence of the Vatican's response to those little pink triangles pinned to the chests of homosexuals imprisoned in the Nazis' concentration camps.

So, here in rapid summary are the 'nos':

No to the 'excessively benevolent interpretations of the homosexual condition';

No 'to the erroneous doctrines regarding homosexuality';

No 'to a new reading of the holy scripture which might attribute to the bible some kind of approval of or lack of condemnation of homosexuality';

No to pressure groups which 'either ignore the teaching of the Church or attempt somehow to subvert it';

No to any meeting under the auspices of Catholicism 'of homosexual persons who have No intention of giving up their homosexual behaviour';

No to attempts 'to change civil statutes';

No to any concession according to which 'homosexuality is at least a completely harmless if not entirely good thing';

No to the opinion that 'homosexual activity could be considered equivalent to, or at least as acceptable as, the sexual expression of love between a married couple';

No to any questioning of the view that 'the homosexual condition is disordered';

No to 'such programmes that attempt to put pressure on the Church to change its doctrine';

No to pastoral programmes which include 'organizations in which homosexuals associate with each other';

No to 'theological opinions which are contrary to the teaching of the Church';

No to any 'organization whatsoever which attempts to subvert the teaching of the Church'.

So, after this letter, what is left to homosexuals who seek refuge in the arms of the Catholic Church? Silence or pretence. Life-long concealment. A life of chastity. This is what millions have suffered and continue to suffer inside the moralistic cage of Catholic doctrine.

In our hero's long career, from Bavaria to the papacy, there have been some crucial moments of transition.

The first was the Second Vatican Council.[8] Ratzinger descends on Rome as a special expert in the retinue of his powerful German bishop. Ratzy's a bit of a lefty, in tune, let's say, with the future 'Sixty-eighters', seeing as the Council is the Roman Church's equivalent of the 1968 student and worker rebellions. But in the course of the revolution, Ratzinger abandons its innovative ideas and emerges from Vatican II as a fierce conservative. He soon attaches himself to Don Giussani and *Comunione e Liberazione*.[9]

---

8   Between 1962 and 1965, convened by pope John XXIII, the reforming pope.

9   *Comunione e Liberazione* [Communion and Liberation]: a traditionalist, integralist lay ecclesiastic movement within the Roman Catholic Church, founded by Monsignor Giussani.

It is the major turning point in his life. And it is through them and Opus Dei[10] that he will eventually reach the papal throne.

The other crucial moment, which is less talked about, is the new catechism; a masterpiece, which he writes while he is Prefect of the Congregation of the Doctrine of the Faith. It is a lucid, well-argued work, an absolute killer. A world bestseller.

So what is the substance of his masterpiece, the new catechism?

Let's have a look at what concerns us, leaving it to every parent, even Catholic ones – especially Catholic ones – to read the whole thing so that they think twice before they place their children in the care of such an ideology:

Subsection 2354 contains the chapter on pornography, which we spare you.

Subsection 2355 contains the chapter on prostitution, and you can imagine what that's like.

Anti-communist in origin, it believes that the law should reflect the teachings of the church.

10   Opus Dei [God's Work]: influential traditionalist organization founded in 1928 in Madrid by Escrivà de Balaguer, now operating worldwide. Membership is mostly lay but includes priests, bishops and cardinals. Pope John Paul II designated it a special order, directly accountable to him. In 2002, he made Escrivà a saint.

Subsection 2356 is on rape. (Do you remember the nuns who were raped and then forced to give birth?).

Subsection 2357, have a guess what this is? But of course, the 'disordered orientation', what else? Homosexuality, under the title of 'Chastity and Homosexuality' is covered in subsection 2357 and subsequent sections. For those of you poor wretches who had to put up with the impositions of the catechism when you were too young to think and for those among you who are lucky enough never to have heard of its existence, we quote in full these particular subsections because, we believe, they speak for themselves to thinking people.

> *2357.* Homosexuality refers to relations between men or between women who experience an exclusive or predominant sexual attraction toward persons of the same sex. It has taken a great variety of forms through the centuries and in different cultures. Its psychological genesis remains largely unexplained. Basing itself on Sacred Scripture, which presents homosexual acts as acts of grave depravity, tradition has always declared that 'homosexual acts are intrinsically disordered.' They are contrary to the natural law. They close the sexual act to the gift of life. They do not proceed from a genuine affective and sexual complementarity. Under no

circumstances can they be approved. [From the authorized English version; see Appendix 3]

A few comments are needed here. The declaration that 'its psychological genesis remains largely unexplained' is pathetic. This is a sleight of hand designed to set up what comes next, the Sacred Scripture in capital letters, and then Tradition (but what tradition?) with a capital T. All this in order to ram down our throats the notion of homosexuality as seriously depraved and 'disordered'. You would need a linguist to explain the latter adjective, and you would be told that in the context of the catechism it is extremely ambiguous and at the same time denigratory, with no room for appeal. As for the law that the catechism proclaims as natural – which is to say, its own law – and on the basis of which it rejects and condemns gays, the reader can see this for what it is. It's obvious that gays can't produce children, but it is also well known that they are willing to adopt, in a world where children have lost their parents through war and epidemics. And the Church in its cruelty (stupidity?) doesn't want that.

As for the 'genuine affective and sexual comple-mentarity', you tell me, dear readers, what on earth that is supposed to mean.

2358. The number of men and women who have deep-seated homosexual tendencies is not negligible. This inclination, which is objectively disordered, constitutes for most of them a trial. They must be accepted with respect, compassion, and sensitivity. Every sign of unjust discrimination in their regard should be avoided. These persons are called to fulfil God's will in their lives and, if they are Christians, to unite to the sacrifice of the Lord's Cross the difficulties they may encounter from their condition ...

Just one comment here: if you are gay and Catholic, suffer, remain chaste, hide away, keep quiet, lie.

2359. Homosexual persons are called to chastity. By the virtues of self-mastery that teach them inner freedom, at times by the support of disinterested friendship, by prayer and sacramental grace, they can and should gradually and resolutely approach Christian perfection.

Please note the stupendous manner in which our inquisitor's text moves from that 'can and should' and that 'gradually and resolutely' to arrive at 'the perfect Christianity', whatever that is; truly a little masterpiece. Worthy of a bestseller, even if reading it is compulsory.

The years go by, and Ratzy takes on liberation theology. Meanwhile, the gay movement grows in strength everywhere, in Italy and all over the world.

24 November 2002

A piece written by the inquisitor sounds like the call to an anti-homosexual crusade to face down the rising gay rights movement. In particular this little excerpt:

> A kind of cultural relativism exists today, evident in the conceptualization and defence of an ethical pluralism, which sanctions the decadence and disintegration of reason and the principles of the natural moral law. Furthermore, it is not unusual to hear the opinion expressed in the public sphere that such ethical pluralism is the very condition for democracy. As a result, citizens claim complete autonomy with regard to their moral choices, and lawmakers maintain they are respecting this freedom of choice by enacting laws which ignore the principles of natural ethics and yield to ephemeral cultural and moral trends, as if every possible outlook on life were of equal

value. At the same time, the value of tolerance is disingenuously invoked when a large number of citizens, Catholics among them, are asked not to base their contribution to society and political life – through the legitimate means available to everyone in a democracy – on their particular understanding of the human person and the common good. The history of the XXth century demonstrates that those citizens were right who recognized the falsehood of relativism, and with it, the notion that there is no moral law rooted in the nature of the human person, which must govern our understanding of man, the common good and the state.

Such relativism, of course, has nothing to do with the legitimate freedom of Catholic citizens to choose among the various political opinions that are compatible with faith and the natural moral law, and to select, according to their own criteria, what best corresponds to the needs of the common good. Political freedom is not – and cannot be – based upon the relativistic idea that all conceptions of the person's good have the same value and the same truth ... [from *Some Questions Regarding the Participation of Catholics in Political Life*, Section II, 21 Nov., 2002; see Appendix 4].

The integralist concept,[11] as banal as it is dangerous, was the underlying premise of another document published at the end of July 2003. It was called 'Considerations Regarding Proposals to Give Legal Recognition to Unions Between Homosexual Persons'. The word 'Considerations' in the title probably means the pope didn't really approve of the contents and had put up some resistance. In the end he obviously gave in and let the document come out on the quiet, without the help of the press and when 'everybody was away at the seaside' at the end of July in Rome. Our hero doesn't usually deny himself the chance to interfere in how the faithful behave in the political life of the country:

> Faced with legislative proposals in favour of homosexual unions, Catholic politicians are to take account of the following ethical indications. When legislation in favour of the recognition of homosexual unions is proposed for the first

---

11 Catholic integralism is anti-pluralist and holds that there is only one true Church, and that all social and political action should be underpinned by catholic teaching. It does not believe in the separation of State and Church; in Italy in the mid-nineteenth century the integralist movement worked to eliminate all competing ideologies, especially Marxism and secular humanism.

time in a legislative assembly, the Catholic law-maker has a moral duty to express his opposition clearly and publicly and to vote against it ... When legislation in favour of the recognition of homosexual unions is already in force, the Catholic politician must oppose it in the ways that are possible for him and make his opposition known ... If it is not possible to repeal such a law completely, the Catholic politician ... could licitly support proposals aimed at limiting the harm done by such a law and at lessening its negative consequences at the level of general opinion and public morality, on condition that his absolute personal opposition to such laws was clear [see Appendix 5].

By now, as well as the key man at Opus Dei, Ratzinger is the power behind the throne of the sick pope and so he begins to dictate the line and consolidate the network which will lift him to the highest Catholic office. Once again the underlying premise is to defend the family at all costs. The defence of the family and the right to life will be the twin pillars of his election campaign.

16 January 2003

This is what he has to say about the family:

> The care and promotion of the family, founded on monogamous marriage between persons of the opposite sex, must be safeguarded. The unity and safety of the family must be defended and protected in the face of modern laws on divorce: other forms of cohabiting cannot be given equal legal status nor as such can they be given legal recognition ... [see also Appendix 4, section 2,4].

13 May 2004

In a speech in the Senate library, in the *Sala Capitolare del Chiostro della Minerva*, our hero went on the attack, in front of the politicians, leaving no room for doubt about his position:

> In blatant contrast to all that, there is the demand for cohabitation between homosexuals, who now paradoxically are asking for some sort of legal status, which must become more or less equivalent to marriage. With this move we are abandoning the whole of the moral history of humanity, which,

despite all the diverse legal forms of marriage, has always recognized that marriage was, in its essence, the particular communion between a man and a woman, which is open to the possibility of children and therefore the family. This is not discrimination, but rather concerns what the human person is, man or woman, and how the coming together of a man and a woman can be granted legal status. If on the one hand their being together increasingly moves away from legal forms, if on the other homosexual union is increasingly seen as having the same status as marriage, we are then facing the destruction of the very image of mankind, the consequences of which can only be extremely serious.

The obscurantism becomes so extreme it cannot be gainsaid. Reasoning becomes pure incitement to paranoia: beware, if you open up just a little bit, then the floodgates will open. Sodom and Gomorrah will follow.

31 May 2004

In a Letter to Catholic Bishops on the collaboration between men and women in the Church and in the world, he returns to the theme of women's liberation, berating this, too, as the antechamber to disaster:

In this perspective, physical difference, termed sex, is minimized, while the purely cultural element, termed gender, is emphasized to the maximum and held to be primary. The obscuring of the difference or duality of the sexes has enormous consequences on a variety of levels. This theory of the human person, intended to promote prospects for equality of women through liberation from biological determinism, has in reality inspired ideologies which, for example, call into question the family, in its natural two-parent structure of mother and father, and make homosexuality and heterosexuality virtually equivalent, in a new model of polymorphous sexuality [authorized translation].

The example of the Spanish PM Zapatero, who found a secular solution for those who want to ratify their union, mainly for practical reasons, opened up a crack that had to be filled in at all costs in our own little backyard.

3 June 2004

Marriage is sacred, whereas homosexual relations go against natural moral law. Homosexual acts, in fact, preclude the gift of life from the sexual act.

They are not the fruit of true affective and sexual complementarity. They cannot in any way be approved of.

Nor do homosexual unions even in the remotely analogous sense carry out the tasks for which marriage and the family merit specific, official recognition. There are, on the other hand, good reasons for maintaining that such unions are a danger to the proper development of human society, especially if their influence on the fabric of society were to increase.

Legal recognition of homosexual unions or making them equivalent to marriage would mean not only approving of deviant behaviour, consequently making it a model available to present society, but also overshadowing the fundamental values which are part of the common heritage of humanity.

19 November 2004

Ratzinger is interviewed by Marco Politi in *La Repubblica*:

Q. *So in your judgment the choice made by Spain is a bad one?*

Yes, because it is destructive, for the family and for society. The law is the basis of morality or a form of morality, since normal people generally believe that what the law decrees is also morally right. And if we judge this type of union to be more or less the equivalent of marriage, we have a society which no longer recognizes the special nature and fundamental characteristic of the family, that is the essence of a man and a woman, which has the aim of maintaining the continuity – not just in the biological sense – of humanity. That's why the choice made in Spain does not really benefit these people: since in this way we are destroying fundamental elements of the legal order.

Q. *Your Holiness, at times in the past when the Church has said no to everything it has been defeated. Should it not at least be possible to allow a pact of solidarity between two people, even homosexuals, which is recognized and protected by the law?*

But the institutionalizing of such an agreement – whether the legislator wants it or not – would of necessity look like just another type of marriage to the public and its relativization would be inevitable. Let's not forget as well that with these kinds of choices, where Europe today seems to be leaning – let's say – towards decadence, we are cutting ourselves off from all the great cultures of humanity, which have always recognized the proper significance of sexuality: namely that a man and a woman were created in order to be together the guarantors of the future of humanity. Not just the physical guarantors but moral as well.

So back into the fray comes the old habit of splitting hairs in four for the easily satisfied readers of *La Repubblica*, for whom a few airy-fairy subtleties are enough to justify total opposition.

But we don't want to bore you any longer on this.

Ratzinger is elected pope at the fourth ballot. In reality the outcome had been decided years ago. The Polish pope had smoothed the way for him by revolutionizing the number of cardinals and choosing the most reactionary ones. And he had practically placed the papal throne in the hands of Opus Dei, in readiness for the restoration which he hadn't had the heart to complete himself, leaving it to his successor, the inquisitor.

There were South American nuns and priests in St Peter's who wept, with good reason, when our hero was elected at the fourth puff of smoke. The first three had been white:[12] delaying the result for the sake of decency, so as not to reveal how well the restoration had been planned for or how solid and uncontested the outcome had been. It was a restoration that was as wretched and depressing as it was inevitable.

And so it was that the little priest with the squeaky voice and the German accent – which sounds a bit like the remnants of Wojtiła's Polish accent, but worse – with a flash of histrionic genius, lifts up his head, throws back his shoulders and finally emerges from the shadows of more than twenty years of obscure, cruel service. He has been waiting for this moment for a decade.

The man is past seventy and is as certain of what he wants as any other doctrinarian and absolutist worth his salt. And now he is the pope! He wisely adopts a humble demeanour in front of the indispensable TV cameras. But he is intelligent, like an old provincial solicitor well versed in the writing of codicils, in the construction of texts stuffed with syllogisms, phrases so inextricably interlocked that they are impossible to refute. These skills were enough for the inquisitor. Will they be enough for the pope?

*

---

12   White smoke means that no-one has yet been elected; black means there is a new pope.

He has now left the little flat in Borgo Pio, which had become sad and lonely after the nun who was his housekeeper died. His neighbour had been a Columbian colleague, Dario Catillon Hoyos, who, like Ratzy, had a piano. But the two never played together and they never socialized. Our hero is a lone wolf, the most solitary pope the Vatican can recall. He's most at ease in his own company. This isolation starts with the 7 a.m. mass (with his beloved Georg). This mass was packed out during the twenty-seven years of Karol Wojtiła's papacy. Now it's reserved for a select few. Whereas mealtimes were social occasions for John Paul II, the new pope sits down at the dining table alone with Georg. The sisters of Memores Domini prepare the often frugal meal. Simplicity above all else. Even in his food. A first course of Viennese consommé, followed by a wooden platter of cold meats, a piece of strudel or a slice of *sachertorte* for dessert. All washed down with the usual Fanta, preferably the low-calorie type, which Ratzinger loves to drink even between meals. Pink grapefruit and *bresaola* are also among his favourite foods. Every now and then he returns to the food of his homeland, Bavaria: *Knödel* in broth and smoked meats. He doesn't turn down a good plate of pasta, either, such as *penne all'arrabbiata*, really spicy, or rice, which has to come exclusively from Vercelli. Solitary and frugal, in short. He once wrote poetry which, unlike his predecessor, he has spared us. All we know is that his poems are about nature and religious feast days.

There's no more leaving home with his wretched leather briefcase containing the little bag of food he gives to the cats along the way, murmuring terms of endearment in his Bavarian dialect, in a show of humanity denied the men in his Church. No more solitary suppers at table six in the Tiroler Keller, the Tyrolean trattoria in Borgo Pio, a short distance from home and the Vatican walls. No more living in cramped rooms which could barely hold his Bavarian furniture and the upright piano on which he played his beloved Mozart and a smattering of Beethoven, and on which he systematically botched Brahms, who his brother had always been on better terms with.

Now there's Georg, who had already been looking after him for a couple of years before Ratzy rose to the papacy. Georg sells the car and organizes the new home: the snazzy flat on the third floor of the apostolic palace, decorated, without thought to the cost, in warm colours that cover the more timid shades, with ultra-modern furniture and above all a high-tech kitchen complete with state-of-the-art appliances straight out of *Elle Decor*.

And there is a piano here, as well of course as one

in the papal summer residence in Castel Gandolfo, just outside Rome, and in the chalet in the Alps.

And in the new, well-appointed home, as in the numerous little Bavarian cottages, there is the inevitable pair of beautiful china cats.

Besides Georg, looking after the new pope is the butler Angelo Gugel and two lay sisters from the Memores Domini, one of whom, Cristina, is a familiar face from when she worked with Ratzinger when he was still a cardinal.

In short, everything has changed. Everything, that is, bar the doctrinal intransigence, the plaintive, strident voice and the crooked mouth, turned down on one side in a perennial grimace. (From how far back? Could it be the result of a facelift that was botched? We don't know. Maybe only Georg knows.)

In the beginning, the declarations of the new pope seem a bit feeble and, above all, too focused on the old mantra of 'God, Country and Family'; this is not very appealing, not very enjoyable. It doesn't have much purchase. That's how it seems, but it won't last long.

His accession to the papal throne fired up his homophobia and produced a fierce attachment to the principle of the sanctity of the family and its position as the natural basic unit of society, as anti-historical an assertion as it was retrograde. His stance on this subject requires the imposition of obsolete rules (no to condoms, no to abortion, no to divorce, no to euthanasia) in clear contrast to the individualism that the West has made its own, along with its products and patterns of consumption.

> Marriage and the family are rooted in the most intimate nucleus of the truth about man and his destiny. This is a legacy which is not simply a combination of doctrine and ideas, but first of all it is an illuminating and unifying lesson on the meaning of human love and life ... and all individualistic concepts of love, so widespread today, must be overcome.

But this outburst on love is just the beginning of a series of declarations which will deal with the sanctity of life.

24 December 2006

Ratzy speaks:

> As far as the sanctity of life is concerned, it is our duty to denounce the destruction of this principle which is being carried out in our society: as well as the victims of armed conflicts, of terrorism and various forms of violence, there are the silent deaths caused by famine, by abortion, by experiments on embryos and by euthanasia. How can we not see all this as a threat to peace?

So, No to abortion, No to condoms. Yes only to procreation according to canon law. All we need now is for him to condemn all sexual positions other than missionary! The concept of life as a 'gift from God', to be cared for according to His demands, leads to tough rules. There are no exceptions.

> The protection of the new-born demands the same urgent attention: we must be careful that pregnant women who find themselves in difficult

circumstances are not denied practical help, and avoid the introduction of drugs which somehow conceal the seriousness of abortion as a choice which is anti-life.

Christian families must bear witness, also through public commitment, to the fundamental values of the Christian faith, such as the inviolability of human life, from conception to its natural end, and the unique and irreplaceable value of the family founded on marriage.

It is of vital importance to communicate the message that fidelity in marriage and abstinence outside it are the best way to avoid infection and the spread of Aids.

This is one of his first public statements, as pope. He seems to have immediately chosen the path of doctrinal intransigence, which is matched with his constant and petulant interference in social life. His pronouncements are tinged with sex phobia as well as homophobia. And typically he straightaway seeks media coverage for the battle, and finds it.

The debate about civil partnerships (*Pacs*), which the Italian parliament is about to accept, provides the perfect opportunity to sound off. There's already the example of Zapatero's Spain.

The Italian press genuflects and pricks up its ears, politicians of Right and Left behave like jackasses. The horizons of the ecumenical Pole are rapidly closing in with dizzying speed. Ratzy turns doctrine into a politico-journalistic weapon which is quickly given ample space and coverage in the *Italietta*[13] of the Berlusconi-ites, who are trying their frenzied hardest to take Italy back to the Middle Ages.

Soon, in speech after speech, it becomes apparent that the pope is after nothing less than the dismantling of the little that remains of Vatican Council II and the complete restoration of the old order. Twenty years of inquisition provided the bare bones which now take on substance, flesh. He has also hit on a cunning way to exploit the paranoia created by the media about Islamic integralism, which in response summons up Catholic integralism (Ornella Fallaci was one of the first people to be received by the pope, just before she died).[14]

---

13   *Italietta*: literally, 'little Italy'; a derogatory term, first used to describe the weak Italian state in the period after the Risorgimento up to and including Giolitti's pre-fascist government.

14   Ornella Fallaci (1929–2006): controversial journalist, war correspondent and writer. She became an outspoken critic of Islam after 9/11 and in 2001 in *Corriere della Sera* she published a piece of invective in which she used, for the first time in Italian, the expression 'clash of civilizations'. This was later republished in *La Rabbia e L'Orgoglio* ('Rage and Pride'), Rizzoli, 2001.

Exploiting the ideological and moral vacuum of Italian politics, the pope attacks divorce, brings back the pre-Council liturgy, claims the absolute and eternal primacy of Rome and reasserts the 'naturalness' of his positions to the exclusion of all others.

Then he really blows it.

Pope Ratzinger, being the professor he is, chose a lecture at his old University of Regensburg to express his views on Islam more explicitly than ever before. He ventured into a learned and inaccessible discourse, which was perhaps ambiguous but certainly inopportune at a time when the words 'clash of civilizations' sound as sinister in the East as they do in the West.

The much-debated passage from that address is a quotation from Manuel II Paleologus, one of the last Byzantine emperors, a learned man and a humanist *ante litteram*. In a dialogue, he says to his interlocutor:

> Show me just what Muhammad brought that was new and there you will find things only evil and inhuman, such as his command to spread by the sword the faith he preached.

Obviously the world press took up the quote as if it were the pope's own words. And they left out the fact that Ratzinger qualified the passage, introducing it by saying, 'He, in a surprisingly brusque manner which is astonishing . . .' and concluded: 'the emperor, having expressed himself in such a heavy-handed manner . . .' It's back to the same old thing, the classic style of the one-time inquisitor who throws the stone and then withdraws his hand. But the stone that is thrown hits an impatient, furious Islam. And the stain remains on the papal hand.

Then we get a growing number of speeches nagging away at the pathetic, wretched little Italian state, and the wretched Right climbs aboard and the terrified excuse for a left-wing covers itself in ashes and bows down as soon as it can in front of the authority it had previously resisted. The civil partnerships (*Pacs*) become a set of rights and obligations (*Dico*),[15] and they in turn end up as a typical Italian fudge. So the feeble voice becomes an endless, unstoppable ejaculatory flow, and the press scoops up every last drop.

And here we are today.

---

15 *Dico*: *Diritti e doveri delle coppie conviventi* (Rights and Obligations of Co-habiting Couples).

2

The Rise and Rise of Georg Gänswein

Georg Gänswein was born on 30 July 1956 in the Black Forest in Riedern am Wald, Landkreis Waldshut, a little village in the lower part of Ratzy's native Bavaria.

He studied in Freiburg im Breisgau, or Freiburg as we know it, then, like all the best and most promising priests from the provinces of the papal empire, he was sent to study canon law in Rome, where he remained for five years at the University of Santa Croce.

It's the start of an amazing career.

Georg possesses a fine, quick intelligence, a great ability to synthesize ideas, and an exceptional physique, which he neither shows off nor hides. And he has an elegantly elitist, traditionalist view of the Church (just like Ratzy).

Rara avis

Georg is an extremely rare bird in the drab environment of the young black, white and yellow priests put through the Vatican theological mill, and superbly adept at what is spiritually politically correct.

Then he returns to Germany to finish his studies at the University of Munich.

On his fiftieth birthday he is still handsome, super-intelligent and very successful. Vatican Radio asks him in German about his youth and about girls, providing him with the perfect goal-scoring opportunity he has been waiting for since the first rumours began to circulate about his 'special friendship' with the old pope. This is what he says:

> I have never had a problem with the so-called weaker sex. I have always had and still have a serene and very natural relationship [with them]. Naturally, when I was young there were girls that I was happy to see, some more than others.

This is just enough to let us know that he is not gay, without committing himself one jot: sublime!

During his years in Bavaria, he frequents the most conservative groups that the most conservative region could provide. And he quickly makes his choices. In Écône, Switzerland, he draws close to the followers of Lefèbvre, founder of the traditionalist, extreme right-wing group the Priestly Fraternity of St Pius X. Although at the time its members are technically heretics, they are much loved by Ratzy, who will later do his utmost to bring them back into the fold. Georg frequents the salons of the murky Bavarian aristocracy, then those of Switzerland and Luxemburg, Belgium and Liechtenstein.

Well-built, with brooding, photogenic good looks, he networks to further his career. He tramps the carpets at the top salons of Northern Europe's right-wing bigots and, as athletic as he is seductive, he keeps up his tennis (he has an excellent volley), football and skiing, for which he wins cups and tournaments at

the exclusive Ski Club of St Anton am Arlberg, in the Austrian Alps.

When he inevitably arrives at Opus Dei, he is a rising star, and with the group's help he reaches dizzying heights. He frequents conservative gatherings and is active on the far Right.

He has contacts with the followers of Plinio Corrêa de Oliveira, founder of the Brazilian Society for the Defence of Tradition, the Family and Property (Sociedade Brasileira de Defesa da Tradição, Família e Propriedade) – quite an agenda. He frequents the Bavarian princely family of Thurn und Taxis, the top people at the Istituto di Cristo Re Sommo Sacerdote and Monsignor Camille Perl, the charismatic secretary of the Papal Commission Ecclesia Dei, which was set up by John Paul II in 1988. Its task is

> To collaborate with the bishops, the Ministries of the Roman Curia and interested circles, with the aim of facilitating the complete ecclesiastic communion of the priests, seminarists, religious communities and individuals up till now linked in various ways to the Fraternity founded by Monsignor Marcel Lefèbvre, who wish to remain united with the Successor to Peter in the Catholic Church.

Georg has always been in the good graces of the bishop of Freiburg im Breisgau, Monsignor Oskar Saier, and those of the archbishop of Cologne. And it is with their blessing that he returns to Rome as a teacher of canon law at the University of Santa Croce, the academic domain of Opus Dei. His career never deviates; it is straight as an arrow, black as pitch.

He goes to live in the German college of Santa Maria della Pietà in Camposanto dei Teutonici, the German institution inside the Vatican which enjoys double extra-territoriality. The German college, as its Italian name suggests, incorporates an extraordinary cemetery (*camposanto*) peopled by dark spectres from the North – German, Austrian, Swiss and Belgian – among them Ludwig Kaas, the pro-Nazi president of the Zentrum, the German Centre Party, at the end of the Weimar Republic, and sister Pasqualina Lehnert, the famous cardinal secretary of state under Pope Pacelli (Pius XII). It is the dark heart of the Vatican.

And guess who celebrates mass each week in the church of Santa Maria in the German college? The prefect of the Congregation for the Doctrine of the Faith, Cardinal Ratzinger.

A few years go by. Don Gänswein is still charming, and as German as can be. Ratzy sees him, takes note. The empathy is immediate. In the light of what follows, we could say that Ratzy is an admirer of the dashing Georg.

The man is handsome, à la Steve McQueen

© Getty Images News

His cassock, impeccably and obsessively ironed, has eighty-six buttonholes and eighty-six buttons, all buttoned up with the patience of a Carthusian monk. And that's not all. The man possesses a quick, versatile intelligence, is attentive, obliging and, perhaps the most important talent of all, he is linked to the most reactionary wing ever to thrive within the Church of St Peter.

He is clearly destined to rise in the Vatican environment, which can be a harsh one; ascent is exclusively via internal routes and requires cunning, good positioning, climbing partners to support him on the way up, and patrons. Our man once lacked a patron: now he has found him.

By now Georg has impeccable, superb, unique advantages as he climbs the most reactionary slopes of a church which, with the exuberant Polish pope in the lead, leaves well behind it what little fresh air Vatican Council II had let in. Wojtiła plays politics, splits communist Poland, attacks exhausted communist Eastern Europe and sets off triumphantly on his transcendent global marketing tours. At home he leaves a little man with a squeaky voice who is difficult to understand; who hits out and destroys every single example of liberation theology reform; who calls in the theologians who don't toe the line, sends his private secretary to meet them at Fiumicino Airport, invites them in for discussions and then pushes them to the margins, condemns them and forces them to leave.

It's 1996

Joseph Ratzinger is approaching seventy and is at the start of his long march to power inside the church directorate. He gradually imposes himself as Pope John Paul II's health declines, and he will rise, appearing before the media clothed in a sort of spiritual asceticism, like a great actor essaying his final role.

Georg is forty years old. He has found his climbing partner. He has found his *padrino* (master, protector, friend? In the Vatican, the subtlety of the games played makes these words too crude). Georg begins work at the Congregation for the Doctrine of the Faith. He is made a second-rank secretary, which means secretary to the private secretary to the cardinal prefect, Ratzy; and guess what? His new boss, Monsignor Josef Clemens, detests Georg. Why has the *padrino* put him in this difficult position?

The extremely clever, extremely accomplished, extremely subtle Ratzy has made the first move in a game of human chess, the probable outcome of which he, Clemens and Georg know in advance.

Don Georg, true to his nature, makes contact with the murky Roman nobility, and given his physique, which is perfect for the part, and his Germanic aplomb, quickly becomes their darling: fêted, flattered, courted. He works for himself, he works for the man whose secretary he is, but above all for the *capo del suo capo* (the boss of his boss). He organizes masses entirely in Latin, in special churches, for the Roman aristocracy.[1] Officiating at these almost secret ceremonies is Cardinal Ratzinger.

---

1   The use of Latin had given way to the use of the vernacular after Vatican Council II, though it had never been abolished. As Pope Benedict, Ratzinger later gave all priests permission to celebrate mass in Latin and encouraged the use of the pre-conciliar liturgy.

There follow four years of Latin masses – officially frowned on by the Church, but in reality symbolic of a particular conception of the Church that Ratzy loves and cultivates. Then in 1986 the meeting in Assisi takes place. This ecumenical curtain raiser, which brings the representatives of other religions together to pray with the pontiff, leaves Ratzinger cold. In an act of almost open rebellion, he refuses to participate. By now he has become strong enough to oppose an ecumenical position which he does not share. In his view, there is only one church, one sole Christ, one sole doctrine. It is said that there was a clash between the pope and his prefect and, even though little emerged from the corridors of the Vatican, that Ratzy was forced to withdraw his objections.

The disagreement was fierce, even though the inquisitor was only doing his job; as was Wojtiła the ecumenical communicator. Deep down the two complemented each other perfectly.

Our Georg, in the meantime, week after week, Latin mass after Latin mass, gains the friendship and affection of the extremely powerful inquisitor. Georg has always paid attention to detail, but now he adds a note of devotion as private secretary to the private secretary. And he soon receives his reward: in 2000, at forty-four years of age, he becomes monsignor. There is no doubt in our mind that it was Ratzy's doing.

Three years go by. It is now November 2004. The Pole is nearing the end. A Monsignor Clemens, private secretary to the cardinal prefect for a full nineteen years and bishop since 6 January 2004, is suddenly promoted to the position of secretary to the Pontifical Council for the Laity. He had shown no previous interest in the job and no one knows what he'll be able to bring to it after so many years of honourable service in the Congregation of the Doctrine of the Faith.

So why on earth did it come about? What can Monsignor Clemens have done to merit such a post? It's not that difficult for our poor Clemens to understand: it's a question of *promuoveatur ut amoveatur*.[2] Ratzy doesn't want him any more. He wants Georg, and he wants him enough to risk exposing his motives.

Monsignor Gänswein, or rather Georg, or rather Ciorcio – as Ratzy pronounces his name in Italian – has finally reached his goal: he is the new private secretary to Ratzinger. (Or is it Ratzinger who has

---

2   A sort of Peter Principle: promoting someone in order to get rid of them.

reached his goal, having moved his beautiful knight around for ten years in an elegant game of chess? Or have they both won, which hardly ever happens in the Vatican?)

Two years later and it's the papal throne

The departing secretary and the handsome incoming secretary quarrel theatrically in the antechambers right next to the papal apartments, *coram populo*, like furious fishwives. The bone of contention: the categorical refusal of Don Giorgio, as the pope's young right-hand man is called in Rome, to give his private mobile phone number to Monsignor Clemens. And it was he who, purple with rage at the snub, started the disconcerting scene. Is this a classic jealous tantrum triggered by a pretext?

Their quarrel ended up in the newspapers during Ratzy's election, which was totally unheard of. The election was never in any doubt, seeing how over the last few years Ratzy had been the real power behind the throne, along with Navarro Valls, the pope's spokesman (and a former Opus Dei journalist), the ultra-conservative Cardinal Ruini and a couple of other very powerful cardinals, as untouchable as they were reactionary.

On the Sunday following his election as pope, after

the mass, Ratzinger sits the handsome priest next to him in his Popemobile and takes him around St Peter's Square to greet the faithful. And so begins the idyll which Ratzy has been preparing for such a long time.

Our two heroes are always together now, at breakfast in the morning, at lunch, again in the afternoon

© Getty Images News

and then on holiday. What they have in common, apart from their reactionary sentiments, many reactionary friends and the thousands of little habits created by their day-to-day contact, is a profound and implacable homophobia.

3

A Sartorial Coming-Out

For fifty-three years, in his black cassock and black beret, Ratzy has been perfectly anonymous as the inquisitor who strikes in the shadows and from there condemns the priests and bishops who, in the clear light of day in South America, fight poverty and tyranny. In a scruffy leather briefcase he carries his verdicts (oh so elegantly worded) which sentence his adversaries to silence; and every day he travels a few hundred metres from his apartment in Borgo Pio to his office in the Vatican.

What can a poor, inflexible little man, by now nearing eighty, do when, after years of interminable, cruel waiting, he becomes, at last and forever, pope of the Holy Roman Church?

On the afternoon of 17 April 2005, protected as always by his black cassock, he slipped quietly out of his house. He was just one of the many priests who wandered around the walls of the Vatican. He entered

through St Anne's Door and reached the Conclave. He left it as pope.

At last he gets to wear white! The three cassocks prepared by Gammarelli, the old tailor's shop which has served the popes since 1792, were blinding white. None of the three fitted our hero. He was forced to wear the least awful of the trio. But he looked ridiculous; the cassock didn't even reach his ankles. And you could see a funny black jumper sticking out from his sleeves.

It is a well-known fact that there is no heating in the Conclave's Sistine Chapel, and so it is an extremely cold pope who emerges to greet *urbi et orbi*, the city and the world. Everybody saw him live and on TV. And TV is unforgiving. His first white cassock probably reminded him of an altar boy's. Gammarelli is quickly punished – or rather 'relieved of his role'. But not officially, for heaven's sake, not officially. The holy inquisitor's *distinguo* will come good and will also be very useful to the new pope, dressed in white. Just in white?

Not for long, not for long.

What can a poor old thing who feels overshadowed by the colossal media profile of his predecessor do? He will never be able to compete with it, or equal it. What else can he do, we mean, other than offer his own depressing, backward vision and the doctrinal inflexibility which has already struck on innumerable occasions? What can he do?

Maybe his adoring batman, the young secretary Ratzy had wanted so much, his suave, strong-willed daily companion, can advise him. Maybe the man with the impeccable, perfectly ironed cassock with its eighty-six buttons will give him some good advice.

The first move is to drop the historic Gammarelli and turn to Alessandro Cattaneo, the head of Euroclero, a company that was created almost at the same time as Ratzy's black cassock, twenty years ago.

When each pope dies, as everyone knows, everything changes so that nothing changes.

A few months go by and Navarro Valls, the pope's elegant, powerful spokesman, leaves of his own free will. Georg is the only person left, and he handles the papers that arrive in the papal apartments and, as his spokesman, makes the pope's views known. And he remains, above all, the arbiter of the sartorial revolution, which is the only thing that can be trusted to make an otherwise lugubrious pope happy.

Soon, in the Roman sunshine, we get the new pope's first, subdued declarations, which reiterate the usual obsessions, starting with his absolutism condemning the relativism of others. Then, soon after this, we get the Ray-Bans: a modern, youthful design, with large wrap-around lenses, which he shows off during public outings whenever it is not raining. This is quite a shock! A pope who is nearly eighty wearing Ray-Bans? The story does the rounds of the world's press.

In the words of the 1968 French slogan, *Ce n'est qu'un début*: it's just the beginning. He has found his media strategy. It will be a combination of doctrinal rigidity and flamboyant dress.

During his holidays in the foothills of the Alps with his dear Ciorcio, an incredible little white baseball cap, its peak pulled down over his forehead, suddenly makes its appearance. As the two of them took their walks together, maybe Georg suggested, proposed (insisted on?) the padded outdoor jacket for him to wear over his white cassock.

Now it's time to start the marketing campaign.

First comes the four-wheel-drive BMW X5; basically it's just a car from Bavaria, they say. Then we have the Geox shoes, which, like the pope, have ecumenical ambitions to conquer the world. The founder, the shrewd Mario Moretti Polegato, had asked his (screwed) friend Navarro Valls to be part of the firm's 'ethical committee'.

By now the international marketing business has realized that the pope, while on the one hand condemning homosexuality as disordered, research on embryos as dangerous, and euthanasia as a mortal sin, is on the other taking more and more risks with

his designer look: sunglasses by Serengeti Bushnell, even an iPod Nano, and then the famous red Prada shoes – flirtatious as never before – all of which make you suspect a deliberate desire to shock and, maybe, a subtle way of mocking those who are beginning to whisper about the special relationship with the handsome Ciorcio.

Then there are the gold cufflinks and the somewhat flashy gold ring of the Fisherman.

Conservatives keep quiet, but the Vatican and Roman rumour-mongers start whispering. Word is the pope's gay. He certainly adopts the outward signs. What if it's all a game? Maybe it's a nonchalance triggered by proximity to his trusted Ciorcio that gives

him at almost eighty the enthusiasm, the passion, for such extreme sartorial risk-taking?

The end of the more relaxed summer holiday season does not bring greater sobriety or better judgment. It becomes obvious to the media, from CNN to the Catholic *l'Avvenire* and the Vatican's *l'Osservatore Romano,* that his sartorial tastes are not a tactic, nor just a bit of fun. They are a strong public statement: a strategy worked out at half-past-seven in the morning over breakfast with his friend, with the ever-present Ciorcio, perhaps, or in the evening ... or thought up between the two of them on holiday.

On 8 December, the Feast of the Immaculate Conception, the pope presents himself in Piazza di Spagna for the traditional visit to the statue of the Madonna near the Spanish Steps. He is wearing a red hat trimmed with ermine. His appearance is both ridiculous and a triumph at the same time: he looks like Father Christmas. What a deliciously dangerous balance between the harshness of his utterances and the gayness of his clothes!

By now even the armoured BMW is part of his reckless and, you could even say, arrogant game, fruit of Georg's intelligence, the man who always looked after everything – the new apartment, the old Volkswagen and the new BMW. And why not also the most spectacular of his hats? The *camauro*, a fur-trimmed cap, dates back to the Middle Ages, and you can see one in the portrait of Julius II by Raphael. Even the beloved 'good pope', John XXIII, had himself painted wearing the *camauro*, but he was the exact opposite of our hero. This pope, on the other hand, with his flashy attire, continues to find new targets to shoot at. Now it's abortion and condoms. Like his predecessor, he continues to condemn the use of condoms in Africa, and in doing so helps to spread the HIV virus, as you know. That's right, because the little man in the big red hats still believes that there is only one way to fight Aids, and that's chastity – total abstinence from any carnal act. Hetero- or homosexual, whatever.

2 March 2006 – from nogod.com

Quick change of clothes for the pope

Spectacular Ash Wednesday ceremony yesterday in Rome. On the long catwalk between St Alessio and St Sabina the pope wore a robe of 'Valentino red' with showy gold embroidery. In the blink of an eye he then appeared in blue à la 'madonna's mantle' ('Renato Balestra' blue, according to the frivolous ladies present),[1] the detailing carrying

---

1   Valentino Garavani (1932–): Italian fashion designer famous for his use of a particular shade of red; Renato Balestra (1924–): Italian fashion designer.

a hint of silver which, depending on the lighting, masterfully controlled by a great set designer, created the effect of 'silver rain drops' on the grey-blue cape. Other experts however talked of a 'silvery dew'. All the altar boys and the host of youthful priests who animated the spectacular ceremony were all dressed in colours to match. Every single outing by Benedict XVI stands out thanks to the richness, the variety and the originality of his clothes, as when in December he showed off the 'camauro', a bizarre piece of headgear in red velvet decorated with cosy ermine.

The man is obviously convinced that he has found the right way to impose himself on the media, without actually bursting through the screen. In writing this book, I consulted several psychologists to learn how far his exuberance in dress was in contrast to his rigid vision of God, that implacable and unfailing doctrine that has taken him to the top, but they weren't very helpful. Nor could they shed much light on the relationship, which seems to go back a long way, between his homophobia and those clearly demonstrated feelings for the very Georg he now shows off to the whole world with such subtle, underhand, mocking pleasure.

Certainly, there can't be a single person who

© MAX ROSSI/Reuters/Corbis

doesn't wonder how such homophobia has the nerve to parade itself day by day alongside that 'handsome man', as even the wife of our former president called him. Some people talk about *The Thornbirds* (*Uccelli di rovo*), Colleen McCullough's novel about a priest who fathers a child. It's quite astonishing that Italy's media wits, such as the writer and journalist Alberto Arbasino, haven't yet made some public quip, since rumours have been circulating for some time in the canteens at RAI, the Italian state broadcaster. But what do you expect? The media in our servile *Italietta* always keep quiet about the truly powerful. Always.

There was, however, a nice piece in *L'espresso* which was quite amusing; every now and then it remembers with a start the good old days when it was a proper magazine. It's worth quoting in full.

No pope, least of all a theologian with a past history as an inflexible custodian of orthodoxy, should be seen wearing padded shoulders, for example, which make him pull back and straighten his shoulders and look metaphorically combative and authoritarian (as opposed to round shoulders, which par excellence signify – not only in papal iconography – calm, meekness and pliability; in short, evangelicalism even!).

This vainglorious, old class-conscious detail which displays so little humility is inspired by Opus Dei and Franco's Spain. It comes from the provocatively anti-modern custom in operas of dressing (or decking out) priests in the long-discarded cassock. Incidentally, far from being

© MAX ROSSI/Reuters/Corbis

apostolic it actually derives, more prosaically, from the sixteenth-century tunic that everyone, including the clergy, at that time wore over their shirt with a bow, waistcoat and culottes, just like a jacket. But for the solemn followers of Escrivà de Balaguer, in an environment where the more comfortable, so-called civilian style of dress [black suit, shirt and white dog-collar] was preferred – and was perfect moreover for immersing oneself wholeheartedly in real life and the here and now – the antiquated form of dress, in certain aspects repellent, had become the unmistakable sign of dissent and of distancing oneself from everything that had been debated and decided in the Vatican Council. In fact, in practice, the clearest refusal of what, in a formulation that will become widely used, was and still is disparagingly called 'the Church of the Left'.

Then we have the most recent ineffable example, the 'camauro', which was such a bad idea and looked as if it was designed on purpose to make Benedict XVI look silly; and a pretty 'saturno' (with a wide brim), in flame red purest moleskin, but more in the improbable style of Pius XI. Exactly like some of the headgear that the Grand Tour has handed down to us in the drawings and paintings of the eighteenth century. This had already been the case, at the 'enthronement' ceremony, with the German antique-dealer pope's choice of a pallium, copied from the one found after a quick search in Tours, no less, on the venerated body of Martin, the old bishop of that city. Together with the Fisherman's ring, again large and flashy. And copes, chasubles and mitres of such heavy gold, so rash and Wagnerian almost as if they had been invented by the infelicitous imagination of Ludwig II of Bavaria. Who on earth, in any case, would be able to decode the tiny allusions to transcendence, hidden away as they were behind the ugly materials and the pastiche?

But by now, like some sort of archaeological curiosity, we have the reappearance of a tiny hood, stylized and miniaturized by the centuries, on the 'mozzetta' (a little ruby red cape in velvet or silk), dug up for the occasion, and the hint of a border in fake ermine. This is in keeping with the complex strategy, involving some kind of plastic-reconstructive surgery, adopted by the Bavarian theologian-cum-aesthete. And nothing can prevent us drawing the cast-iron conclusion that here is a pope who, once an expert at the Vatican Council, has completely distanced himself from it. Our conclusion is backed up by his irrepressible propensity for aestheticizing, nostalgic sentimentalism and rigid rule from the top which seem to be the foundational elements of the cultural structure of this papacy (geography, stylistically speaking, always prevails over history).

Meanwhile, all around, people have more or less reached the same conclusions as Stendhal: they picture woolly-thinking, ambitious priests and vain bishops. As in a disapproving painting by Meissonier.[2] And at the top: straight, rigid shoulders. Held up by two simple shoulder pads – a bit like roofing tiles – jutting out dangerously in order to support him, stylistically speaking of course, under the pure white innocuous cassock of the pope. Who has very clear ideas in his head. And a parading of mitred bishops the likes of which we had not seen since the ecclesiastical fashion show put on by Danilo Donati and Federico Fellini in the film *Roma*. But then it was just pretend. So, what is the style? Neo-Neuschwanstein, it would seem. Like the final, melodramatic eccentricity of the unhappy Ludwig, king of Bavaria.

27 November 2006

---

2   Ernest Meissonier (1815–1891): French painter.

In the meantime, our hero seems to be seeking constant, direct confrontation with the gay community, which by now has its own saints in the press, the electronic media and parliament. Conflict is to his taste, as was shown when he found an indirect vent for his views on Islam. The German 'blunder' was nothing of the sort, and it would be an insult to his keen and at times sublime intelligence to think it was. The retraction that followed was barely credible and few took it at face value.

So clothes seem to have become the only opportunity for fun in an otherwise incessant, coruscating series of outbursts against *Pacs* (civil partnerships), against a supine government which waters them down to become *Dico* (an agreement on rights and obligations) and then further dilutes them until they are practically meaningless.

And then comes the most theatrical appearance of all, which we will let someone who was there describe:

The pink pope[3]

Glorious in a flashy pink chasuble, today the pope demonstrated yet again his extraordinary ability to dress in the most original and showy tent-like clothes and headgear. But on today's visit to the juvenile prison at Casal del Marno it wasn't so much the chasuble which struck commentators and the faithful and made them snigger, but the unusually dazzling colour of what he was wearing: a lovely shiny tea-rose pink which made his fleshy ivory-coloured cheeks seem more transparent than ever. Obviously the resulting faint pink reflection helped considerably to mitigate the depth of the wrinkles, the horrible ravages of age on the sacred pontifical skin. What was also extraordinary was the way the chasuble matched to perfection the purple decorations and vestments typically worn during Lent. There is great disquiet among the top stylists, who have no idea who is the designer responsible for suggesting to the Vatican tailors the

---

3   See http://www.nessundio.net/vaticanfashion.htm

cut and the nuances of the clothes, the decorations and set design.

18 March 2007

It's a Sartorial Coming-Out

© Stefano Spaziani

Papal Details

SUNGLASSES
One of the aesthetic changes Ratzinger has made: the use of sunglasses, even during meetings in public.

CUFFLINKS
Pope Benedict XVI loves wearing gold cufflinks

THE RING
On his right hand, the gold ring of the Fisherman, with the papal seal.

THE TAILOR
The white woollen cassock, designed by Euroclero. It has a front opening with no less than thirty buttons

THE MOCCASINS
According to the English newspaper the *Independent*, the red shoes worn by the pope are by Prada.

Orazio La Rocca, 'Il look di papa Ratzinger: spuntano le scarpe Prada' ['Pope Razinger's look: Prada shoes have appeared'], *La Repubblica* (5 November 2005)

4

The Greatest Gay Pope
(Not the Only One)

Giovanni Maria Ciocchi del Monte (1487–
1555), later pope Julius III, studies law at
Perugia and Bologna. He then devotes himself to
an ecclesiastic career, at that time maybe the most
attractive choice next to going to war (which he often
saw as one and the same). He becomes archbishop
of Siponto[1] and a very capable and manipulative
diplomat, as well as a man of culture and patron
to equal the popes who preceded him. These were
Clement VII Medici and Paul III Farnese, with
whom he worked closely. He is made cardinal in
1536.

It is his ability to manoeuvre that in 1550 takes
him to the papacy, where he has to negotiate his

---

1   Siponto: ancient port city in Apulia, Southern Italy, aban-
doned after earthquakes in the thirteenth century.

way between the empire to which he is allied and a powerful, arrogant France. He is still a cardinal when the Pasquinate – that is, the writings left at the statue of Pasquino, which is still there behind Piazza Navona (but no one writes on it nowadays) – describe him as a great sodomite. A sodomite cardinal is one thing (normal, in fact), but a sodomite pope is quite another, especially one who is fully outed.

Four months after he is elected pope, Julius III makes his young lover, Innocenzo del Monte (1532–1577), who is seventeen years old (sound familiar?), a cardinal. He had fallen in love with the boy, called Santino, the son of one of his servants, when the lad was thirteen and Julius had practically bought him in exchange for substantial favours. When Santino was fourteen, Julius III granted him a number of church benefices. Later he persuaded his brother Baldovino to adopt the boy.

It was a story of great passion of epic length. It was the period of the Council of Trent and the counter-offensive launched by the Church of Rome in order to check the advance of the Reformation. The Curia put up some resistance to the nomination of the extremely young cardinal. But Julius III was in love, and he was, as they say, deaf in that ear.

And I am certainly not prepared to condemn him for such a powerful love. It was said of Santino that

he looked after the pope's monkey, and so he was called Bertuccina.[2] The Venetian ambassador Matteo Dandolo wrote that he was a 'little scoundrel' and that a cardinal (when still a cardinal) took him into his bedroom and into his bed as if he had been his son or his nephew. An elegant if poisonous comment on

---

2 *Bertuccia* means Barbary ape in Italian. *Uccia* and *ina* are diminutive suffixes, hence *Bertuccina*: it sounds like a girl's name meaning 'pretty little Berta'.

the decision made by the future Julius III to make Santino his adopted nephew.

The courts of Europe bad-mouthed the pope, laughed and were shocked, but Rome had seen it all before, and worse, and they treated him in the same way they always treated their pope-kings: cursing, mocking, surviving, and above all patiently putting up with the worst government in Europe and the dissolute flesh-pit of a court.

Julius III was no worse than many other popes. He continued to protect Michelangelo and to support the Compagnia di Gesù, which he allowed to build the Roman College and the German College. He built up the Vatican library, extended the University of La Sapienza, and built Villa Giulia, which now houses the Etruscan Museum, while also finding time to work for the ascendancy of Mary the Catholic, otherwise known as Bloody Mary, to the throne of England.

It was Santino, who was given the name Innocenzo when he was made cardinal, who came out of it badly. When Julius III died, after only five years as pope, Santino, who by now was twenty-three, went on the rampage. He was involved in a series of rapes, acts of violence and homicides. But in the end, despite everything, he was buried next to his pope (at least for them a sort of posthumous Renaissance civil partnership worked out).

5

To the Secular Reader Concerning the Less than Infallible Ratzinger

As you will have guessed, I do not share the views of those who need some sort of God in order to find within themselves a moral code, a vision of the world, past, present or future. Nor of those superficial and hypocritical people who pretend to believe in an abstract God because it is the done thing, or because they are afraid of the afterlife or, even worse, an obsolete hell.

We will leave this world, for the last time we imagine, curious to know what lies in that undiscovered country, from whose shores no traveller returns. As for hell – about which our hero said pathetically: *Hell exists and is eternal, even if hardly anyone talks about it any more* – we are left with the wonderful verses of Dante: *Ove udirai le disperate strida / vedrai li antichi spiriti dolenti* (Where you hear desperate cries / you will see ancient spirits who are suffering) – verses which have become part of our poetic imagination.[1]

Our infallible little man, entranced, as he recounts, by his vestments, the sounds, the pomp of a church in Bavaria, has led a life filled with indestructible certainties, structured around and consolidated by his studies of ancient incontrovertible texts, which had to be learned and annotated but never refuted.

The fear of a Marxism that demanded paradise on earth cast a dark shadow over the whole of his life. Every sign of charity towards the poor and the rejected on the part of more open-minded and generous clerics became a reason to be hostile, to condemn and to marginalize.

The thinking secularist, whose mind is not clouded by absolutes, by Kantian critique, might ask whether there is a link between the visceral rejection of those who are 'different' and the uncharitable and categorical description of them as 'disordered', and the even worse argument that homosexuals bring about dissipation, hence the 'not unjustified' discrimination. This was in a world that in the meantime was learning tolerance and respect and therefore accepted those very same homosexuals, men and women, who represent one-tenth of the population everywhere under the sun

---

1   The quote is from *The Divine Comedy*, Inferno, Canto 1.

and are subject to every more or less cruel, more or less tolerant God that history has left us as a legacy.

The secularist will inevitably wonder, not particularly maliciously, whether such fury isn't the fruit of a deeply repressed desire for what he condemns. Of an unconscious desire which manifests itself as its opposite. We note the twenty years he spent issuing condemnations in the name of an absolute. And we wonder how far that attitude could be the result of some blockage in his heart, an impediment to his feelings, something troubling his conscience.

© Alessandra Benedetti/Corbis

Now that he has ascended to the throne, our hero has discovered the dazzling clothes, the trappings of power and wealth, which centuries of pomp have draped on the shoulders of his predecessors. In this way, his true nature, his deepest unspoken inclinations are revealed. In short, he might simply be the most repressed, imploded gay in the world. And here he is, with his young protégé standing by him, letting rip in Prada shoes and fancy accessories. Does the showiness of the Ray-Bans, a little incongruous for a man of nearly eighty, hide a gleam in his eye?

Everything leads us to believe that the man is finally giving vent to his true gay nature. And in the wide-brimmed flame-red hat, in the Father Christmas beret, in the lovely pink chasuble worn during a visit to a prison, he expresses – not in the flesh, which might no longer be an option, but at least visually, at least as a spectacle – his true personality, which has remained hidden away behind the pre-papal grey mask of the dusty scholar and fierce inquisitor. About ten years before he became pope, when age was beginning to take its toll and was maybe sharpening the secret internal rage, Ratzy met Don Giorgio. And it was a spark of life amid the doctrinal darkness.

We poor mortal secularists, who feel the Socratic God inside us, believe that love is a mixture of

the carnal and the metaphysical, of coupling and sentiment, climaxes of the imagination as well as the body. We could never experience the purely mental dizzying *coup de foudre* of the chaste man, of the virginal man who has never touched a woman or even a man (or so we assume).

We have all read St Theresa of Ávila; we have seen the evocative statue by Bernini, the little cherub with his golden arrow, the mystical and carnal ecstasy so wonderfully rendered.[2] So we can at least imagine

---

2 St Theresa of Ávila (1515–1582): Spanish saint; Lorenzo

how a pure soul becomes inflamed when it meets its soul mate, when a nearly seventy-year-old prefect of the Congregation for the Doctrine of the Faith meets a brilliant forty-year-old priest from his native Bavaria who shares the same outlook on the world.

We understand and, full of compassion, we empathize. And we are able, with our different and less rarefied understanding of 'special friendships', to feel moved by their human story and to understand it. To grasp their pleasure in being close, their day-to-day lives together, their sharing of problems and solutions, dangers and judgments, holidays in the mountains and ceremonies in the city.

But then we have a real moral problem.

When we see the photos, which we publish in this book, of Georg putting Ratzy's little hat on for him, handing him his stole, watching his back, looking after him, accompanying him and helping him as he walks, we cannot help being moved. And yet we know that here we are dealing with the man who destroyed liberation theology, who continues undaunted to forbid condoms to those who need them in order not to die from Aids, and to deny divorce to his

---

Bernini (1598–1680): his statue is part of the altar in a side chapel in the Santa Maria della Vittoria church in Rome; it depicts her 'heavenly rapture' when an angel pierces her heart.

poor subjects. Even if these things go back a long way, to dozens of popes who did even worse things, those who have a secular understanding of justice, intellectual honesty and emotional clarity still find them reprehensible, dreadful.

We know that this is the man who condemns abortion because it 'goes against nature' and who does not wish to know how painful it is for a woman to abort, especially in secret. We know that this is the man who talks about the sanctity of marriage when he knows full well that the great patriarchal family is finished; and that the nuclear family is the offspring of a capitalism that tells us to produce, consume and die, and obviously uses condoms, which by now are sold on every street corner despite the fact that he still insists they are sinful.

Basically we all know – us and him – that he is spitting in the wind. That he is setting himself up as a Taliban against other Taliban gods. But we cannot forget how his vision of 'pain which redeems', like that of St Theresa of Calcutta, means that in our hypocritical, supine Italian society the sick and suffering are not given enough morphine and that even today people are made to suffer pointlessly. Nor can we forget that his tireless, relentless preaching that our lives do not belong to us but to God means that believers don't even have the right to end their own lives how and when they want, as Petronius did in a warm bath when he opened his veins, or as poor tormented Welby, tired of and sickened by his non-life, wanted.[3]

Now we don't wish to, and maybe we shouldn't, enter into that old debate, nor the countless others in which we find our position markedly different from the pope's, from that of all popes. It's enough to dip into a smattering of the doctrines of control bequeathed to us after 2000 years of Church

---

3   Gaius Petronius, author of *The Satyricon*, died in CE 65; Piergiorgio Welby (1945–2006): Italian poet, painter and campaigner for the right to die. He suffered from muscular dystrophy and fought for three months to be allowed to die, eventually winning that right. This led to a wide debate about euthanasia in Italy.

pontificating (consider the derivation of that word) – doctrines that are all-encompassing and totally political, all about power, all about a Church that, alas, has preferred pomp, sex phobia and repression to the charity of its Christ. We wonder instead whether our hero's stubborn, persistent and personal homophobia comes from a self-repression that is so deep that it is unequalled (he is the pope, after all) on land or sea.

In this book, as an example, we refer to a pope who was homosexual, not only in orientation but also in deeds. And what deeds! And we say this because our hero always distinguishes in his accusatory pronounce-ments, as is the case in all confessions, between orientation, and the actual deed, the sin committed.

But if, as we secularists believe, hell and sin are

just ancient visions of a crude imagination, now superseded like the paradise of the houri,[4] then let the compassion within us assert itself. And in spite of all the damage done down the centuries by the Church of which he is the head, we are unable to judge or even less condemn an old man sitting on that demanding, impossible throne, who has found in himself, after years of loneliness, a rush of empathy that we like to call human love.

Far be it from us to distinguish between intention and act.

Be it consummated love or not, be it a deep mutual understanding, whether it is a loving friendship, whether it is affection, personal and intellectual understanding, whether it is one of the thousand and one nuances in feelings which literature has described and celebrated countless times, we respect what he feels, despite everything.

And if tradition and catholic doctrine want to confine the love that is consummated between a man and a woman to the narrow space they call marriage, we on the other hand call the love between a man and a woman, between a man and a man, between a woman and a woman, love without distinction. And we fervently hope that the serotonin of consonance

---

4   Houri: a nymph in the Muslim version of paradise.

and affection he has discovered for the other may loosen the knots of sad inflexibility, as it has before in even the hardest of hearts. That our hero, who knows, may come to understand that it is his Ego, not his God, that judges and condemns a human, only too human, form of love.

Description of an Idyllic Day in Georg's Own Words

(radio interview transcript)

> The pope's day begins with the seven o'clock mass, then he says prayers with his breviary, followed by a period of silent contemplation before our Lord. Then we have breakfast together, and so I begin the day's work by going through the correspondence. Then I exchange ideas with the Holy Father, then I accompany him to the 'Second Loggia' for the private midday audiences. Then we have lunch together; after the meal we go for a little walk before taking a nap. In the afternoon I again take care of correspondence. I take the most important stuff which needs his signature to the Holy Father.

With regard to the day-to-day relationship with the pope, Don Georg explains: 'I try to show myself worthy of his trust: after a year and three months our ability to work together has grown.' When asked, 'Do you still feel nervous when you find yourself in the presence of the Holy Father?' he replies that, though he is used to 'being in the spotlight' that inevitably surrounds the pope, he sometimes does. He adds:

> But it is also true that the fact of meeting each other and being together on a daily basis creates a sense of 'familiarity', which makes you feel less nervous. But obviously I know who the Holy Father is and so I know how to behave appropriately. There are always some situations, however, when the heart beats a little stronger than usual.

© Mihai Romanciuc

The top placard reads: Joseph and Georg we are fighting for you, too. The banner below reads: The Pope is gay like us.

Photos taken on 10 March 2007, during the pro-DICO demonstration when 50,000 people flocked to Piazza Farnese and Campo de' Fiori, where Giordano Bruno was burned at the stake and the only square in the centre of Rome without a church.

Appendices

The Vatican's Position on Homosexualtiy as Detailed
by the Congregation for the Doctrine of the Faith

Appendix 1

Letter to the Bishops of the Catholic Church on
the Pastoral Care of Homosexual Persons

1. The issue of homosexuality and the moral evaluation of homosexual acts have increasingly become a matter of public debate, even in Catholic circles. Since this debate often advances arguments and makes assertions inconsistent with the teaching of the Catholic Church, it is quite rightly a cause for concern to all engaged in the pastoral ministry, and this Congregation has judged it to be of sufficiently grave and widespread importance to address to the Bishops of the Catholic Church this Letter on the Pastoral Care of Homosexual Persons.

2. Naturally, an exhaustive treatment of this complex issue cannot be attempted here, but we will focus our reflection within the distinctive context of the Catholic moral perspective. It is a perspective which finds support in the more secure findings of the

natural sciences, which have their own legitimate and proper methodology and field of inquiry.

However, the Catholic moral viewpoint is founded on human reason illumined by faith and is consciously motivated by the desire to do the will of God our Father. The Church is thus in a position to learn from scientific discovery but also to transcend the horizons of science and to be confident that her more global vision does greater justice to the rich reality of the human person in his spiritual and physical dimensions, created by God and heir, by grace, to eternal life.

It is within this context, then, that it can be clearly seen that the phenomenon of homosexuality, complex as it is, and with its many consequences for society and ecclesial life, is a proper focus for the Church's pastoral care. It thus requires of her ministers attentive study, active concern and honest, theologically well-balanced counsel.

3. Explicit treatment of the problem was given in this Congregation's 'Declaration on Certain Questions Concerning Sexual Ethics' of December 29, 1975. That document stressed the duty of trying to understand the homosexual condition and noted that culpability for homosexual acts should only be judged with prudence. At the same time the Congregation took

note of the distinction commonly drawn between the homosexual condition or tendency and individual homosexual actions. These were described as deprived of their essential and indispensable finality, as being 'intrinsically disordered', and able in no case to be approved of (cf. n. 8, §4).

In the discussion which followed the publication of the Declaration, however, an overly benign interpretation was given to the homosexual condition itself, some going so far as to call it neutral, or even good. Although the particular inclination of the homosexual person is not a sin, it is a more or less strong tendency ordered toward an intrinsic moral evil; and thus the inclination itself must be seen as an objective disorder.

Therefore special concern and pastoral attention should be directed toward those who have this condition, lest they be led to believe that the living out of this orientation in homosexual activity is a morally acceptable option. It is not.

4. An essential dimension of authentic pastoral care is the identification of causes of confusion regarding the Church's teaching. One is a new exegesis of Sacred Scripture which claims variously that Scripture has nothing to say on the subject of homosexuality, or that it somehow tacitly approves of it, or that all of

its moral injunctions are so culture-bound that they are no longer applicable to contemporary life. These views are gravely erroneous and call for particular attention here.

5. It is quite true that the Biblical literature owes to the different epochs in which it was written a good deal of its varied patterns of thought and expression (Dei Verbum 12). The Church today addresses the Gospel to a world which differs in many ways from ancient days. But the world in which the New Testament was written was already quite diverse [*sic*] from the situation in which the Sacred Scriptures of the Hebrew People had been written or compiled, for example.

What should be noticed is that, in the presence of such remarkable diversity, there is nevertheless a clear consistency within the Scriptures themselves on the moral issue of homosexual behaviour. The Church's doctrine regarding this issue is thus based, not on isolated phrases for facile theological argument, but on the solid foundation of a constant Biblical testimony. The community of faith today, in unbroken continuity with the Jewish and Christian communities within which the ancient Scriptures were written, continues to be nourished by those same Scriptures and by the Spirit of Truth whose Word they are. It is likewise essential to recognize that the Scriptures are not properly understood when they are interpreted in a way which contradicts the Church's living Tradition. To be correct, the interpretation of Scripture must be in substantial accord with that Tradition.

The Vatican Council II in Dei Verbum 10 put it this way: 'It is clear, therefore, that in the supremely wise arrangement of God, sacred Tradition, sacred Scripture, and the Magisterium of the Church are so connected and associated that one of them cannot stand without the others. Working together, each in its own way under the action of the one Holy Spirit, they all contribute effectively to the salvation of souls.' In that spirit we wish to outline briefly the Biblical teaching here.

6. Providing a basic plan for understanding this entire discussion of homosexuality is the theology of creation we find in Genesis. God, in his infinite wisdom and love, brings into existence all of reality as a reflection of his goodness. He fashions mankind, male and female, in his own image and likeness. Human beings, therefore, are nothing less than the work of God himself; and in the complementarity of the sexes, they are called to reflect the inner unity of the Creator. They do this in a striking way in their cooperation with him in the transmission of life by a mutual donation of the self to the other.

In Genesis 3, we find that this truth about persons being an image of God has been obscured by original sin. There inevitably follows a loss of awareness of the covenantal character of the union these persons had with God and with each other. The human body retains its 'spousal significance' but this is now clouded by sin. Thus, in Genesis 19:1–11, the deterioration due to sin continues in the story of the men of Sodom. There can be no doubt of the moral judgement made there against homosexual relations. In Leviticus 18:22 and 20:13, in the course of describing the conditions necessary for belonging to the Chosen People, the author excludes from the People of God those who behave in a homosexual fashion.

Against the background of this exposition of theocratic law, an eschatological perspective is developed by St Paul when, in I Cor 6:9, he proposes the same doctrine and lists those who behave in a homosexual fashion among those who shall not enter the Kingdom of God.

In Romans 1:18–32, still building on the moral traditions of his forebears, but in the new context of the confrontation between Christianity and the pagan society of his day, Paul uses homosexual behaviour as an example of the blindness which has overcome humankind. Instead of the original harmony between Creator and creatures, the acute distortion of idolatry has led to all kinds of moral excess. Paul is at a loss to find a clearer example of this disharmony than homosexual relations. Finally, 1 Tim. 1, in full continuity with the Biblical position, singles out those who spread wrong doctrine and in v. 10 explicitly names as sinners those who engage in homosexual acts.

7. The Church, obedient to the Lord who founded her and gave to her the sacramental life, celebrates the divine plan of the loving and life-giving union of men and women in the sacrament of marriage. It is only in the marital relationship that the use of the sexual faculty can be morally good. A person engaging in homosexual behaviour therefore acts immorally.

To choose someone of the same sex for one's sexual activity is to annul the rich symbolism and meaning, not to mention the goals, of the Creator's sexual design. Homosexual activity is not a complementary union, able to transmit life; and so it thwarts the call to a life of that form of self-giving which the Gospel says is the essence of Christian living. This does not mean that homosexual persons are not often generous and giving of themselves; but when they engage in homosexual activity they confirm within themselves a disordered sexual inclination which is essentially self-indulgent.

As in every moral disorder, homosexual activity prevents one's own fulfilment and happiness by acting contrary to the creative wisdom of God. The Church, in rejecting erroneous opinions regarding homosexuality, does not limit but rather defends personal freedom and dignity realistically and authentically understood.

8. Thus, the Church's teaching today is in organic continuity with the Scriptural perspective and with her own constant Tradition. Though today's world is in many ways quite new, the Christian community senses the profound and lasting bonds which join us to those generations who have gone before us, 'marked with the sign of faith'.

Nevertheless, increasing numbers of people today, even within the Church, are bringing enormous pressure to bear on the Church to accept the homosexual condition as though it were not disordered and to condone homosexual activity. Those within the Church who argue in this fashion often have close ties with those with similar views outside it. These latter groups are guided by a vision opposed to the truth about the human person, which is fully disclosed in the mystery of Christ. They reflect, even if not entirely consciously, a materialistic ideology which denies the transcendent nature of the human person as well as the supernatural vocation of every individual.

The Church's ministers must ensure that homosexual persons in their care will not be misled by this point of view, so profoundly opposed to the teaching of the Church. But the risk is great and there are many who seek to create confusion regarding the Church's position, and then to use that confusion to their own advantage.

9. The movement within the Church, which takes the form of pressure groups of various names and sizes, attempts to give the impression that it represents all homosexual persons who are Catholics. As a matter of fact, its membership is by and large restricted to those who either ignore the teaching of the Church or seek somehow to undermine it. It brings together under the aegis of Catholicism homosexual persons who have no intention of abandoning their homosexual behaviour. One tactic used is to protest that any and all criticism of or reservations about homosexual people, their activity and lifestyle, are simply diverse forms of unjust discrimination.

There is an effort in some countries to manipulate the Church by gaining the often well-intentioned support of her pastors with a view to changing civil statutes and laws. This is done in order to conform to these pressure groups' concept that homosexuality is at least a completely harmless, if not an entirely good, thing. Even when the practice of homosexuality may seriously threaten the lives and well-being of a large number of people, its advocates remain undeterred and refuse to consider the magnitude of the risks involved.

The Church can never be so callous. It is true that her clear position cannot be revised by pressure from civil legislation or the trend of the moment. But she is really concerned about the many who are not represented by the pro-homosexual movement and about those who may have been tempted to believe its deceitful propaganda. She is also aware that the view that homosexual activity is equivalent to, or as acceptable as, the sexual expression of conjugal love has a direct impact on society's understanding of the nature and rights of the family and puts them in jeopardy.

10. It is deplorable that homosexual persons have been and are the object of violent malice in speech or in action. Such treatment deserves condemnation from the Church's pastors wherever it occurs. It reveals a kind of disregard for others which endangers the most fundamental principles of a healthy society. The intrinsic dignity of each person must always be respected in word, in action and in law.

But the proper reaction to crimes committed against homosexual persons should not be to claim that the homosexual condition is not disordered. When such a claim is made and when homosexual activity is consequently condoned, or when civil legislation is introduced to protect behavior to which no one has any conceivable right, neither the Church nor society at large should be surprised when other distorted notions and practices gain ground, and irrational and violent reactions increase.

11. It has been argued that the homosexual orientation in certain cases is not the result of deliberate choice; and so the homosexual person would then have no choice but to behave in a homosexual fashion. Lacking freedom, such a person, even if engaged in homosexual activity, would not be culpable.

Here, the Church's wise moral tradition is necessary since it warns against generalizations in judging individual cases. In fact, circumstances may exist, or may have existed in the past, which would reduce or remove the culpability of the individual in a given instance; or other circumstances may increase it. What is at all costs to be avoided is the unfounded and demeaning assumption that the sexual behaviour of homosexual persons is always and totally compulsive and therefore inculpable. What is essential is that the fundamental liberty which characterizes the human person and gives him his dignity be recognized as belonging to the homosexual person as well. As in every conversion from evil, the abandonment of homosexual activity will require a profound collaboration of the individual with God's liberating grace.

12. What, then, are homosexual persons to do who seek to follow the Lord? Fundamentally, they are called to enact the will of God in their life by joining whatever sufferings and difficulties they experience in virtue of their condition to the sacrifice of the Lord's Cross. That Cross, for the believer, is a fruitful sacrifice since from that death come life and redemption. While any call to carry the cross or to understand a Christian's suffering in this way will predictably be met with bitter ridicule by some, it should be remembered that this is the way to eternal life for all who follow Christ.

It is, in effect, none other than the teaching of Paul the Apostle to the Galatians when he says that the Spirit produces in the lives of the faithful 'love, joy, peace, patience, kindness, goodness, trustfulness, gentleness and self-control' (5:22) and further (v. 24), 'You cannot belong to Christ unless you crucify all self-indulgent passions and desires.'

It is easily misunderstood, however, if it is merely seen as a pointless effort at self-denial. The Cross is a denial of self, but in service to the will of God himself who makes life come from death and empowers those who trust in him to practise virtue in place of vice.

To celebrate the Paschal Mystery, it is necessary to let that Mystery become imprinted in the fabric of daily life. To refuse to sacrifice one's own will in obedience to the will of the Lord is effectively to prevent salvation. Just as the Cross was central to the expression of God's redemptive love for us in Jesus, so the conformity of the self-denial of homosexual men and women with the sacrifice of the Lord will constitute for them a source of self-giving which will save them from a way of life which constantly threatens to destroy them.

Christians who are homosexual are called, as all of us are, to a chaste life. As they dedicate their lives to understanding the nature of God's personal call to them, they will be able to celebrate the Sacrament of Penance more faithfully and receive the Lord's grace so freely offered there in order to convert their lives more fully to his Way.

13. We recognize, of course, that in great measure the clear and successful communication of the Church's teaching to all the faithful, and to society at large,

depends on the correct instruction and fidelity of her pastoral ministers. The Bishops have the particularly grave responsibility to see to it that their assistants in the ministry, above all the priests, are rightly informed and personally disposed to bring the teaching of the Church in its integrity to everyone.

The characteristic concern and good will exhibited by many clergy and religious in their pastoral care for homosexual persons is admirable, and, we hope, will not diminish. Such devoted ministers should have the confidence that they are faithfully following the will of the Lord by encouraging the homosexual person to lead a chaste life and by affirming that person's God-given dignity and worth.

14. With this in mind, this Congregation wishes to ask the Bishops to be especially cautious of any programmes which may seek to pressure the Church to change her teaching, even while claiming not to do so. A careful examination of their public statements and the activities they promote reveals a studied ambiguity by which they attempt to mislead the pastors and the faithful. For example, they may present the teaching of the Magisterium, but only as if it were an optional source for the formation of one's conscience. Its specific authority is not recognized. Some of these groups will use the word 'Catholic' to describe

either the organization or its intended members, yet they do not defend and promote the teaching of the Magisterium; indeed, they even openly attack it. While their members may claim a desire to conform their lives to the teaching of Jesus, in fact they abandon the teaching of his Church. This contradictory action should not have the support of the Bishops in any way.

15. We encourage the Bishops, then, to provide pastoral care in full accord with the teaching of the Church for homosexual persons of their dioceses. No authentic pastoral programme will include organizations in which homosexual persons associate with each other without clearly stating that homosexual activity is immoral. A truly pastoral approach will appreciate the need for homosexual persons to avoid the near occasions of sin.

We would heartily encourage programmes where these dangers are avoided. But we wish to make it clear that departure from the Church's teaching, or silence about it, in an effort to provide pastoral care is neither caring nor pastoral. Only what is true can ultimately be pastoral. The neglect of the Church's position prevents homosexual men and women from receiving the care they need and deserve.

An authentic pastoral programme will assist homosexual persons at all levels of the spiritual life:

through the sacraments, and in particular through the frequent and sincere use of the sacrament of Reconciliation, through prayer, witness, counsel and individual care. In such a way, the entire Christian community can come to recognize its own call to assist its brothers and sisters, without deluding them or isolating them.

16. From this multi-faceted approach there are numerous advantages to be gained, not the least of which is the realization that a homosexual person, as every human being, deeply needs to be nourished at many different levels simultaneously.

The human person, made in the image and likeness of God, can hardly be adequately described by a reductionist reference to his or her sexual orientation. Every one living on the face of the earth has personal problems and difficulties, but challenges to growth, strengths, talents and gifts as well. Today, the Church provides a badly needed context for the care of the human person when she refuses to consider the person as a 'heterosexual' or a 'homosexual' and insists that every person has a fundamental Identity: the creature of God, and by grace, his child and heir to eternal life.

17. In bringing this entire matter to the Bishops' attention, this Congregation wishes to support their

efforts to ensure that the teaching of the Lord and his Church on this important question be communicated fully to all the faithful.

In light of the points made above, they should decide for their own dioceses the extent to which an intervention on their part is indicated. In addition, should they consider it helpful, further coordinated action at the level of their National Bishops' Conference may be envisioned.

In a particular way, we would ask the Bishops to support, with the means at their disposal, the development of appropriate forms of pastoral care for homosexual persons. These would include the assistance of the psychological, sociological and medical sciences, in full accord with the teaching of the Church.

They are encouraged to call on the assistance of all Catholic theologians who, by teaching what the Church teaches, and by deepening their reflections on the true meaning of human sexuality and Christian marriage with the virtues it engenders, will make an important contribution in this particular area of pastoral care.

The Bishops are asked to exercise special care in the selection of pastoral ministers so that by their own high degree of spiritual and personal maturity and by their fidelity to the Magisterium, they may be of real service to homosexual persons, promoting their health and well-being in the fullest sense. Such ministers will reject theological opinions which dissent from the teaching of the Church and which, therefore, cannot be used as guidelines for pastoral care.

We encourage the Bishops to promote appropriate catechetical programmes based on the truth about human sexuality in its relationship to the family as taught by the Church. Such programmes should provide a good context within which to deal with the question of homosexuality.

This catechesis would also assist those families of homosexual persons to deal with this problem which affects them so deeply.

All support should be withdrawn from any organizations which seek to undermine the teaching of the Church, which are ambiguous about it, or which neglect it entirely. Such support, or even the semblance of such support, can be gravely misinterpreted. Special attention should be given to the practice of scheduling religious services and to the use of Church buildings by these groups, including the facilities of Catholic schools and colleges. To some, such permission to use Church property may seem only just and charitable; but in reality it is contradictory to the purpose for which these institutions were founded, it is misleading and often scandalous.

In assessing proposed legislation, the Bishops

should keep as their uppermost concern the responsibility to defend and promote family life.

18. The Lord Jesus promised, 'You shall know the truth and the truth shall set you free' (Jn. 8:32). Scripture bids us speak the truth in love (cf. Eph. 4:15). The God who is at once truth and love calls the Church to minister to every man, woman and child with the pastoral solicitude of our compassionate Lord. It is in this spirit that we have addressed this Letter to the Bishops of the Church, with the hope that it will be of some help as they care for those whose suffering can only be intensified by error and lightened by truth.

(During an audience granted to the undersigned Prefect, His Holiness, Pope John Paul II, approved this Letter, adopted in an ordinary session of the Congregation for the Doctrine of the Faith, and ordered it to be published.)

Given at Rome, 1 October 1986

JOSEPH CARDINAL RATZINGER
Prefect
ALBERTO BOVONE
Titular Archbishop of Caesarea in Numidia Secretary

Appendix 2

Some Considerations Concerning the Response to Legislative Proposals on the Non-Discrimination of Homosexual Persons

Revised statement issued on 22 July 1992

Foreword

Recently, legislation has been proposed in various places which would make discrimination on the basis of sexual orientation illegal. In some cities, municipal authorities have made public housing, otherwise reserved for families, available to homosexual (and unmarried heterosexual) couples. Such initiatives, even where they seem more directed toward support of basic civil rights than condonement of homosexual activity or a homosexual lifestyle, may in fact have a negative impact on the family and society. Such things as the adoption of children, the employment of teachers, the housing needs of genuine families, landlords' legitimate concerns in screening potential tenants, for example, are often implicated.

While it would be impossible to anticipate every eventuality in respect to legislative proposals in this area, these observations will try to identify some principles and distinctions of a general nature which should be taken into consideration by the conscientious legislator, voter, or church authority who is confronted with such issues.

The first section will recall relevant passages from the Congregation for the Doctrine of the Faith's 'Letter to the Bishops of the Catholic Church on the Pastoral Care of Homosexual Persons' of 1986. The second section will deal with their application.

I.   *Relevant Passages from the CDF's 'Letter'*

1. The letter recalls that the CDF's 'Declaration on Certain Questions Concerning Sexual Ethics' of 1975 'took note of the distinction commonly drawn between the homosexual condition or tendency and individual homosexual actions'; the latter are 'intrinsically disordered' and 'in no case to be approved of' (No. 3).

2. Since '[i]n the discussion which followed the publication of the (aforementioned) declaration . . . an overly benign interpretation was given to the homosexual condition itself, some going so far as

to call it 'neutral or even good', the letter goes on to clarify: 'Although the particular inclination of the homosexual person is not a sin, it is a more or less strong tendency ordered toward an intrinsic moral evil; and thus the inclination itself must be seen as an objective disorder. Therefore special concern and pastoral attention should be directed toward those who have this condition, lest they be led to believe that the living out of this orientation in homosexual activity is a morally acceptable option. It is not' (No. 3).

3. 'As in every moral disorder, homosexual activity prevents one's own fulfilment and happiness by acting contrary to the creative wisdom of God. The church, in rejecting erroneous opinions regarding homosexuality, does not limit but rather defends personal freedom and dignity realistically and authentically understood' (No. 7).

4. In reference to the homosexual movement, the letter states: 'One tactic used is to protest that any and all criticism of or reservations about homosexual people, their activity and lifestyle, are simply diverse forms of unjust discrimination' (No. 9).

5. 'There is an effort in some countries to manipulate the church by gaining the often well-intentioned

support of her pastors with a view to changing civil statutes and laws. This is done in order to conform to these pressure groups' concept that homosexuality is at least a completely harmless, if not an entirely good, thing. Even when the practice of homosexuality may seriously threaten the lives and well-being of a large number of people, its advocates remain undeterred and refuse to consider the magnitude of the risks involved' (No. 9).

6. 'She (the church) is also aware that the view that homosexual activity is equivalent to or as acceptable as the sexual expression of conjugal love has a direct impact on society's understanding of the nature and rights of the family and puts them in jeopardy' (No. 9).

7. 'It is deplorable that homosexual persons have been and are the object of violent malice in speech or in action. Such treatment deserves condemnation from the church's pastors wherever it occurs. It reveals a kind of disregard for others which endangers the most fundamental principles of a healthy society. The intrinsic dignity of each person must always be respected in word, in action and in law.

'But the proper reaction to crimes committed against homosexual persons should not be to claim that the homosexual condition is not disordered.

When such a claim is made and when homosexual activity is consequently condoned, or when civil legislation is introduced to protect behaviour to which no one has any conceivable right, neither the church nor society at large should be surprised when other distorted notions and practices gain ground, and irrational and violent reactions increase (No. 10).

8. 'What is at all costs to be avoided is the unfounded and demeaning assumption that the sexual behaviour of homosexual persons is always and totally compulsive and therefore inculpable. What is essential is that the fundamental liberty which characterizes the human person and gives him his dignity be recognized as belonging to the homosexual person as well' (No. 11).

9. 'In assessing proposed legislation, the Bishops should keep as their uppermost concern the responsibility to defend and promote family life' (No. 17).

II.   Applications
10. 'Sexual orientation' does not constitute a quality comparable to race, ethnic background, etc. in respect to non-discrimination. Unlike these, homosexual orientation is an objective disorder (cf. 'Letter,' No. 3) and evokes moral concern.

11. There are areas in which it is not unjust discrimination to take sexual orientation into account, for example, in the placement of children for adoption or foster care, in employment of teachers or athletic coaches, and in military recruitment.

12. Homosexual persons, as human persons, have the same rights as all persons including the right of not being treated in a manner which offends their personal dignity (cf. No. 10). Among other rights, all persons have the right to work, to housing, etc. Nevertheless, these rights are not absolute. They can be legitimately limited for objectively disordered external conduct. This is sometimes not only licit but obligatory. This would obtain moreover not only in the case of culpable behavior but even in the case of actions of the physically or mentally ill. Thus it is accepted that the state may restrict the exercise of rights, for example, in the case of contagious or mentally ill persons, in order to protect the common good.

13. Including 'homosexual orientation' among the considerations on the basis of which it is illegal to discriminate can easily lead to regarding homosexuality as a positive source of human rights, for example, in respect to so-called affirmative action

or preferential treatment in hiring practices. This is all the more deleterious since there is no right to homosexuality (cf. No. 10) which therefore should not form the basis for judicial claims. The passage from the recognition of homosexuality as a factor on which basis it is illegal to discriminate can easily lead, if not automatically, to the legislative protection and promotion of homosexuality. A person's homosexuality would be invoked in opposition to alleged discrimination, and thus the exercise of rights would be defended precisely via the affirmation of the homosexual condition instead of in terms of a violation of basic human rights.

14. The 'sexual orientation' of a person is not comparable to race, sex, age, etc. also for another reason than that given above which warrants attention. An individual's sexual orientation is generally not known to others unless he publicly identifies himself as having this orientation or unless some overt behaviour manifests it. As a rule, the majority of homosexually oriented persons who seek to lead chaste lives do not publicize their sexual orientation. Hence the problem of discrimination in terms of employment, housing, etc., does not usually arise.

Homosexual persons who assert their homosexuality tend to be precisely those who judge homosexual behaviour or lifestyle to be 'either completely harmless, if not an entirely good thing' (cf. No. 3), and hence worthy of public approval. It is from this quarter that one is more likely to find those who seek to 'manipulate the church by gaining the often well-intentioned support of her pastors with a view to changing civil statutes and laws' (cf. No. 5), those who use the tactic of protesting that 'any and all criticism of or reservations about homosexual people . . . are simply diverse forms of unjust discrimination' (cf. No. 9).

In addition, there is a danger that legislation which would make homosexuality a basis for entitlements could actually encourage a person with a homosexual orientation to declare his homosexuality or even to seek a partner in order to exploit the provisions of the law.

15. Since in the assessment of proposed legislation uppermost concern should be given to the responsibility to defend and promote family life (cf. No. 17), strict attention should be paid to the single provisions of proposed measures. How would they affect adoption or foster care? Would they protect homosexual acts, public or private? Do they confer equivalent family status on homosexual unions, for example, in respect to public housing or by

entitling the homosexual partner to the privileges of employment which could include such things as 'family' participation in the health benefits given to employees (cf. No. 9)?

16. Finally, where a matter of the common good is concerned, it is inappropriate for church authorities to endorse or remain neutral toward adverse legislation even if it grants exceptions to church organizations and institutions. The church has the responsibility to promote family life and the public morality of the entire civil society on the basis of fundamental moral values, not simply to protect herself from the application of harmful laws (cf. No. 17).

Appendix 3

Relevant Sections of the 1992 Catechism of the Catholic Church

Article 6: The Sixth Commandment

You shall not commit adultery.[1]

> You have heard that it was said, 'You shall not commit adultery.' But I say to you that every one who looks at a woman lustfully has already committed adultery with her in his heart.[2]

II. The Vocation To Chastity

2337 Chastity means the successful integration of sexuality within the person and thus the inner unity of man in his bodily and spiritual being. Sexuality, in

---

1   EX 20:14; Deut 5:18.
2   Mt 5:27–28

which man's belonging to the bodily and biological world is expressed, becomes personal and truly human when it is integrated into the relationship of one person to another, in the complete and lifelong mutual gift of a man and a woman.

The virtue of chastity therefore involves the integrity of the person and the integrality of the gift.

The integrity of the person

2338 The chaste person maintains the integrity of the powers of life and love placed in him. This integrity ensures the unity of the person; it is opposed to any behaviour that would impair it. It tolerates neither a double life nor duplicity in speech.[3]

2339 Chastity includes an *apprenticeship in self-mastery* which is a training in human freedom. The alternative is clear: either man governs his passions and finds peace, or he lets himself be dominated by them and becomes unhappy.[4] 'Man's dignity therefore requires him to act out of conscious and free choice, as moved and drawn in a personal way from within, and not by blind impulses in himself or by mere external constraint. Man gains such dignity

---

3   Cf. Mt 5:37.
4   Cf. Sir 1:22.

when, ridding himself of all slavery to the passions, he presses forward to his goal by freely choosing what is good and, by his diligence and skill, effectively secures for himself the means suited to this end.'[5]

2340 Whoever wants to remain faithful to his baptismal promises and resist temptations will want to adopt the means for doing so: self-knowledge, practice of an ascesis adapted to the situations that confront him, obedience to God's commandments, exercise of the moral virtues, and fidelity to prayer. 'Indeed it is through chastity that we are gathered together and led back to the unity from which we were fragmented into multiplicity.'[6]

2341 The virtue of chastity comes under the cardinal virtue of *temperance*, which seeks to permeate the passions and appetites of the senses with reason.

2342 Self-mastery is a *long and exacting work*. One can never consider it acquired once and for all. It presupposes renewed effort at all stages of life.[7] The effort required can be more intense in certain periods,

---

5   GS 17.
6   St Augustine, Conf. 10, 29, 40: PL 32, 796.
7   Cf. Titus 2:1–6.

such as when the personality is being formed during childhood and adolescence.

2343 Chastity has *laws of growth* which progress through stages marked by imperfection and too often by sin. 'Man ... day by day builds himself up through his many free decisions; and so he knows, loves, and accomplishes moral good by stages of growth.'[8]

2344 Chastity represents an eminently personal task; it also involves a *cultural effort*, for there is 'an interdependence between personal betterment and the improvement of society.'[9] Chastity presupposes respect for the rights of the person, in particular the right to receive information and an education that respect the moral and spiritual dimensions of human life.

2345 Chastity is a moral virtue. It is also a gift from God, a *grace*, a fruit of spiritual effort.[10] The Holy Spirit enables one whom the water of Baptism has regenerated to imitate the purity of Christ.[11]

---

8 FC 34.
9 GS 25 # 1.
10 Cf. Gal 5:22.
11 Cf. 1 Jn 3:3.

The integrality of the gift of self

2346 Charity is the *form* of all the virtues. Under its influence, chastity appears as a school of the gift of the person. Self-mastery is ordered to the gift of self. Chastity leads him who practises it to become a witness to his neighbour of God's fidelity and loving kindness.

2347 The virtue of chastity blossoms in *friendship*. It shows the disciple how to follow and imitate him who has chosen us as his friends,[12] who has given himself totally to us and allows us to participate in his divine estate. Chastity is a promise of immortality.

Chastity is expressed notably in *friendship with one's neighbour.* Whether it develops between persons of the same or opposite sex, friendship represents a great good for all. It leads to spiritual communion.

The various forms of chastity

2348 All the baptized are called to chastity. The Christian has 'put on Christ',[13] the model for all chastity. All Christ's faithful are called to lead a chaste life in keeping with their particular states of life. At the moment of his Baptism, the Christian is pledged to lead his affective life in chastity.

---

12   Cf. Jn 15:15.
13   Gal 3:27.

2349 'People should cultivate [chastity] in the way that is suited to their state of life. Some profess virginity or consecrated celibacy which enables them to give themselves to God alone with an undivided heart in a remarkable manner. Others live in the way prescribed for all by the moral law, whether they are married or single.'[14] Married people are called to live conjugal chastity; others practise chastity in continence:

> There are three forms of the virtue of chastity: the first is that of spouses, the second that of widows, and the third that of virgins. We do not praise any one of them to the exclusion of the others … This is what makes for the richness of the discipline of the Church.[15]

2350 Those who are *engaged to marry* are called to live chastity in continence. They should see in this time of testing a discovery of mutual respect, an apprenticeship in fidelity, and the hope of receiving one another from God. They should reserve for marriage the expressions of affection that belong to married love. They will help each other grow in chastity.

---

14   CDF, Persona humana 11.
15   St Ambrose, De viduis 4, 23: PL 16, 255A.

Offenses against chastity

2351 *Lust* is disordered desire for or inordinate enjoyment of sexual pleasure. Sexual pleasure is morally disordered when sought for itself, isolated from its procreative and unitive purposes.

2352 By *masturbation* is to be understood the deliberate stimulation of the genital organs in order to derive sexual pleasure. 'Both the Magisterium of the Church, in the course of a constant tradition, and the moral sense of the faithful have been in no doubt and have firmly maintained that masturbation is an intrinsically and gravely disordered action.'[16] 'The deliberate use of the sexual faculty, for whatever reason, outside marriage is essentially contrary to its purpose.' For here sexual pleasure is sought outside of 'the sexual relationship which is demanded by the moral order and in which the total meaning of mutual self-giving and human procreation in the context of true love is achieved'.[17]

To form an equitable judgment about the subjects' moral responsibility and to guide pastoral action, one must take into account the affective immaturity, force of acquired habit, conditions of anxiety or other

---

16   CDF, Persona humana 9.
17   Ibid.

psychological or social factors that lessen, if not even reduce to a minimum, moral culpability.

2353 *Fornication* is carnal union between an unmarried man and an unmarried woman. It is gravely contrary to the dignity of persons and of human sexuality which is naturally ordered to the good of spouses and the generation and education of children. Moreover, it is a grave scandal when there is corruption of the young.

2354 *Pornography* consists in removing real or simulated sexual acts from the intimacy of the partners, in order to display them deliberately to third parties. It offends against chastity because it perverts the conjugal act, the intimate giving of spouses to each other. It does grave injury to the dignity of its participants (actors, vendors, the public), since each one becomes an object of base pleasure and illicit profit for others. It immerses all who are involved in the illusion of a fantasy world. It is a grave offense. Civil authorities should prevent the production and distribution of pornographic materials.

2355 *Prostitution* does injury to the dignity of the person who engages in it, reducing the person to an instrument of sexual pleasure. The one who pays sins gravely against himself: he violates the chastity to which his Baptism pledged him and defiles his body, the temple of the Holy Spirit.[18] Prostitution is a social scourge. It usually involves women, but also men, children, and adolescents. (The latter two cases involve the added sin of scandal.) While it is always gravely sinful to engage in prostitution, the imputability of the offence can be attenuated by destitution, blackmail, or social pressure.

2356 *Rape* is the forcible violation of the sexual intimacy of another person. It does injury to justice and charity. Rape deeply wounds the respect, freedom, and physical and moral integrity to which every person has a right. It causes grave damage that can mark the victim for life. It is always an intrinsically evil act. Graver still is the rape of children committed by parents (incest) or those responsible for the education of the children entrusted to them.

Chastity and homosexuality

2357 Homosexuality refers to relations between men or between women who experience an exclusive or predominant sexual attraction toward persons of the same sex. It has taken a great variety of forms

---

18   Cf. 1 Cor 6:15–20.

through the centuries and in different cultures. Its psychological genesis remains largely unexplained. Basing itself on Sacred Scripture, which presents homosexual acts as acts of grave depravity,[19] tradition has always declared that 'homosexual acts are intrinsically disordered'.[20] They are contrary to the natural law. They close the sexual act to the gift of life. They do not proceed from a genuine affective and sexual complementarity. Under no circumstances can they be approved.

2358 The number of men and women who have deep-seated homosexual tendencies is not negligible. This inclination, which is objectively disordered, constitutes for most of them a trial. They must be accepted with respect, compassion, and sensitivity. Every sign of unjust discrimination in their regard should be avoided. These persons are called to fulfil God's will in their lives and, if they are Christians, to unite to the sacrifice of the Lord's Cross the difficulties they may encounter from their condition.

2359 Homosexual persons are called to chastity. By the virtues of self-mastery that teach them inner

---

19   Cf. Gen 191:29; Rom 124:27; 1 Cor 6:10; 1 Tim 1:10.
20   CDF, Persona humana 8.

freedom, at times by the support of disinterested friendship, by prayer and sacramental grace, they can and should gradually and resolutely approach Christian perfection.

Appendix 4

Doctrinal Note on Some Questions Regarding the Participation of Catholics in Political Life

*The Congregation for the Doctrine of the Faith, having received the opinion of the Pontifical Council for the Laity, has decided that it would be appropriate to publish the present **Doctrinal Note on some questions regarding the participation of Catholics in political life.** This Note is directed to the Bishops of the Catholic Church and, in a particular way, to Catholic politicians and all lay members of the faithful called to participate in the political life of democratic societies.*

I. A constant teaching

1. The commitment of Christians in the world has found a variety of expressions in the course of the past 2000 years. One such expression has been Christian involvement in political life: Christians, as one Early Church writer stated, 'play their full

role as citizens'.[1] Among the saints, the Church venerates many men and women who served God through their generous commitment to politics and government. Among these, Saint Thomas More, who was proclaimed Patron of Statesmen and Politicians, gave witness by his martyrdom to 'the inalienable dignity of the human conscience'.[2] Though subjected to various forms of psychological pressure, Saint Thomas More refused to compromise, never forsaking the 'constant fidelity to legitimate authority and institutions' which distinguished him; he taught by his life and his death that 'man cannot be separated from God, nor politics from morality'.[3]

It is commendable that in today's democratic societies, in a climate of true freedom, everyone is made a participant in directing the body politic.[4] Such societies call for new and fuller forms of participation in public life by Christian and non-Christian citizens alike. Indeed, all can contribute, by voting in elections for lawmakers

---

1   *Letter to Diognetus,* 5,5; Cf. *Catechism of the Catholic Church,* No. 2240.

2   John Paul II, Apostolic Letter Motu Proprio *Proclaiming Saint Thomas More Patron of Statesmen and Politicians,* 1: *AAS* 93 (2001), 76.

3   Ibid., 4.

4   Cf. Second Vatican Council, Pastoral Constitution *Gaudium et spes,* 31; *Catechism of the Catholic Church,* No. 1915.

and government officials, and in other ways as well, to the development of political solutions and legislative choices which, in their opinion, will benefit the common good.[5] The life of a democracy could not be productive without the active, responsible and generous involvement of everyone, 'albeit in a diversity and complementarity of forms, levels, tasks, and responsibilities'.[6]

By fulfilling their civic duties, 'guided by a Christian conscience',[7] in conformity with its values, the lay faithful exercise their proper task of infusing the temporal order with Christian values, all the while respecting the nature and rightful autonomy of that order,[8] and cooperating with other citizens according to their particular competence and

---

5   Cf. Second Vatican Council, Pastoral Constitution *Gaudium et spes*, 75.

6   John Paul II, Apostolic Exhortation, *Christifideles laici,* 42: *AAS* 81 (1989), 472. The present doctrinal *Note* refers to the involvement in political life of lay members of the faithful. The Bishops of the Church have the right and the duty to set out the moral principles relating to the social order; 'Nevertheless active participation in political parties is reserved to the lay faithful' (ibid., 60). Cf. Congregation for the Clergy, *Directory for the Ministry and Life of Priests* (31 March 1994), 33.

7   Second Vatican Council, Pastoral Constitution *Gaudium et spes,* 76.

8   Cf. Second Vatican Council, Pastoral Constitution *Gaudium et spes,* 36.

responsibility.[9] The consequence of this fundamental teaching of the Second Vatican Council is that 'the lay faithful are never to relinquish their participation in "public life", that is, in the many different economic, social, legislative, administrative and cultural areas, which are intended to promote organically and institutionally the common good'.[10] This would include the promotion and defence of goods such as public order and peace, freedom and equality, respect for human life and for the environment, justice and solidarity.

The present *Note* does not seek to set out the entire teaching of the Church on this matter, which is summarized in its essentials in the *Catechism of the Catholic Church,* but intends only to recall some principles proper to the Christian conscience, which inspire the social and political involvement of Catholics in democratic societies.[11] The emergence of

---

9   Cf. Second Vatican Council, Decree *Apostolicam actuositatem,* 7; Dogmatic Constitution *Lumen gentium,* 36; Pastoral Constitution *Gaudium et spes,* 31 and 43.

10   John Paul II, Apostolic Exhortation *Christifideles laici,* 42.

11   In the last two centuries, the Papal Magisterium has spoken on the principal questions regarding the social and political order. Cf. Leo XIII, Encyclical Letter *Diuturnum illud*: *ASS* 14 (1881–1882), 4ff; Encyclical Letter *Immortale Dei*: *ASS* 18 (1885–1886), 162ff; Encyclical Letter *Libertas præstantissimum*: *ASS* 20 (1887–1888), 593ff; Encyclical Letter *Rerum novarum*:

ambiguities or questionable positions in recent times, often because of the pressure of world events, has made it necessary to clarify some important elements of Church teaching in this area.

II. Central points in the current cultural and political debate

2. Civil society today is undergoing a complex cultural process as the end of an era brings with it a time of uncertainty in the face of something new. The great strides made in our time give evidence of humanity's progress in attaining conditions of life which are more in keeping with human dignity. The growth in the sense of responsibility towards countries still on the path of development is without doubt an important sign, illustrative of a greater sensitivity to

---

ASS 23 (1890–1891), 643ff; Benedict XV, Encyclical Letter *Pacem Dei munus pulcherrimum*: AAS 12 (1920), 209ff; Pius XI, Encyclical Letter *Quadragesimo anno*: AAS 23 (1931), 190ff; Encyclical Letter *Mit brennender Sorge*: AAS 29 (1937), 145–167; Encyclical Letter *Divini Redemptoris*: AAS 29 (1937), 78ff; Pius XII, Encyclical Letter *Summi Pontificatus*: AAS 31 (1939), 423ff; *Radiomessaggi natalizi 1941–1944;* John XXIII, Encyclical Letter *Mater et magistra*: AAS 53 (1961), 401–464; Encyclical Letter *Pacem in terris*: AAS 55 (1963), 257–304; Paul VI, Encyclical Letter *Populorum progressio*: AAS 59 (1967), 257–299; Apostolic Letter *Octogesima adveniens*: AAS 63 (1971), 401–441.

the common good. At the same time, however, one cannot close one's eyes to the real dangers which certain tendencies in society are promoting through legislation, nor can one ignore the effects this will have on future generations.

A kind of cultural relativism exists today, evident in the conceptualization and defence of an ethical pluralism, which sanctions the decadence and disintegration of reason and the principles of the natural moral law. Furthermore, it is not unusual to hear the opinion expressed in the public sphere that such ethical pluralism is the very condition for democracy.[12] As a result, citizens claim complete autonomy with regard to their moral choices, and lawmakers maintain that they are respecting this freedom of choice by enacting laws which ignore the principles of natural ethics and yield to ephemeral cultural and moral trends,[13] as if every possible outlook on life were of equal value. At the same time, the value of tolerance is disingenuously invoked when a large number of citizens, Catholics among

---

12   Cf. John Paul II, Encyclical Letter *Centesimus annus,* 46: *AAS* 83 (1991); Encyclical Letter *Veritatis splendor*, 101: *AAS* 85 (1993), 1212–1213; *Discourse to the Italian Parliament,* 5: *L'Osservatore Romano* (November 15, 2002).

13   Cf. John Paul II, Encyclical Letter *Evangelium vitae,* 22: *AAS* 87 (1995), 425–426.

them, are asked not to base their contribution to society and political life – through the legitimate means available to everyone in a democracy – on their particular understanding of the human person and the common good. The history of the twentieth century demonstrates that those citizens were right who recognized the falsehood of relativism, and with it, the notion that there is no moral law rooted in the nature of the human person, which must govern our understanding of man, the common good and the state.

3. Such relativism, of course, has nothing to do with the legitimate freedom of Catholic citizens to choose among the various political opinions that are compatible with faith and the natural moral law, and to select, according to their own criteria, what best corresponds to the needs of the common good. Political freedom is not – and cannot be – based upon the relativistic idea that all conceptions of the human person's good have the same value and truth, but rather, on the fact that politics are concerned with very concrete realizations of the true human and social good in given historical, geographic, economic, technological and cultural contexts. From the specificity of the task at hand and the variety of circumstances, a plurality of morally

acceptable policies and solutions arises. It is not the Church's task to set forth specific political solutions – and even less to propose a single solution as the acceptable one – to temporal questions that God has left to the free and responsible judgment of each person. It is, however, the Church's right and duty to provide a moral judgment on temporal matters when this is required by faith or the moral law.[14] If Christians must 'recognize the legitimacy of differing points of view about the organization of worldly affairs',[15] they are also called to reject, as injurious to democratic life, a conception of pluralism that reflects moral relativism. Democracy must be based on the true and solid foundation of non-negotiable ethical principles, which are the underpinning of life in society.

On the level of concrete political action, there can generally be a plurality of political parties in which Catholics may exercise – especially through legislative assemblies – their right and duty to contribute to the public life of their country.[16] This arises because of the contingent nature of certain choices regarding

---

14   Cf. Second Vatican Council, Pastoral Constitution *Gaudium et spes,* 76.

15   Second Vatican Council, Pastoral Constitution *Gaudium et spes,* 75.

16   Cf. Second Vatican Council, Pastoral Constitution *Gaudium et spes,* 43 and 75.

the ordering of society, the variety of strategies available for accomplishing or guaranteeing the same fundamental value, the possibility of different interpretations of the basic principles of political theory, and the technical complexity of many political problems. It should not be confused, however, with an ambiguous pluralism in the choice of moral principles or essential values. The legitimate plurality of temporal options is at the origin of the commitment of Catholics to politics and relates directly to Christian moral and social teaching. It is in the light of this teaching that lay Catholics must assess their participation in political life so as to be sure that it is marked by a coherent responsibility for temporal reality.

The Church recognizes that while democracy is the best expression of the direct participation of citizens in political choices, it succeeds only to the extent that it is based on a correct understanding of the human *person*.[17] Catholic involvement in political life cannot compromise on this principle, for otherwise the witness of the Christian faith in the world, as well as the unity and interior coherence of the faithful, would be non-existent. The democratic

---

17 Cf. Second Vatican Council, Pastoral Constitution *Gaudium et spes,* 25.

structures on which the modern state is based would be quite fragile were its foundation not the centrality of the human person. It is respect for the person that makes democratic participation possible. As the Second Vatican Council teaches, the protection of 'the rights of the person is, indeed, a necessary condition for citizens, individually and collectively, to play an active part in public life and administration'.[18]

4. The complex array of today's problems branches out from here, including some never faced by past generations. Scientific progress has resulted in advances that are unsettling for the consciences of men and women and call for solutions that respect ethical principles in a coherent and fundamental way. At the same time, legislative proposals are put forward which, heedless of the consequences for the existence and future of human beings with regard to the formation of culture and social behaviour, attack the very inviolability of human life. Catholics, in this difficult situation, have the right and the duty to recall society to a deeper understanding of human life and to the responsibility of everyone in this regard. John Paul II, continuing the constant teaching of the Church,

---

18   Second Vatican Council, Pastoral Constitution *Gaudium et spes*, 73.

has reiterated many times that those who are directly involved in lawmaking bodies have a *'grave and clear obligation to oppose'* any law that attacks human life. For them, as for every Catholic, it is impossible to promote such laws or to vote for them.[19] As John Paul II has taught in his Encyclical Letter *Evangelium vitae* regarding the situation in which it is not possible to overturn or completely repeal a law allowing abortion which is already in force or coming up for a vote, 'an elected official, whose absolute personal opposition to procured abortion was well known, could licitly support proposals aimed at *limiting the harm* done by such a law and at lessening its negative consequences at the level of general opinion and public morality'.[20]

In this context, it must be noted also that a well-formed Christian conscience does not permit one to vote for a political program or an individual law which contradicts the fundamental contents of faith and morals. The Christian faith is an integral unity, and thus it is incoherent to isolate some particular element to the detriment of the whole of Catholic doctrine. A political commitment to a single isolated aspect of the Church's social doctrine does not exhaust one's responsibility towards the common

---

19   Cf. John Paul II, Encyclical Letter *Evangelium vitae,* 73.
20   Ibid.

good. Nor can a Catholic think of delegating his Christian responsibility to others; rather, the Gospel of Jesus Christ gives him this task, so that the truth about man and the world might be proclaimed and put into action.

When political activity comes up against moral principles that do not admit of exception, compromise or derogation, the Catholic commitment becomes more evident and laden with responsibility. In the face of *fundamental and inalienable ethical demands,* Christians must recognize that what is at stake is the essence of the moral law, which concerns the integral good of the human person. This is the case with laws concerning *abortion* and *euthanasia* (not to be confused with the decision to forgo *extraordinary treatments,* which is morally legitimate). Such laws must defend the basic right to life from conception to natural death. In the same way, it is necessary to recall the duty to respect and protect the rights of the *human embryo.* Analogously, the *family* needs to be safeguarded and promoted, based on monogamous marriage between a man and a woman, and protected in its unity and stability in the face of modern laws on divorce: in no way can other forms of cohabitation be placed on the same level as marriage, nor can they receive legal recognition as such. The same is true for the freedom of parents regarding the *education* of their children; it is an inalienable right recognized also by the Universal Declaration on Human Rights. In the same way, one must consider *society's protection of minors* and freedom from *modern forms of slavery* (drug abuse and prostitution, for example). In addition, there is the right to *religious freedom* and the development of an *economy* that is at the service of the human person and of the common good, with respect for social justice, the principles of human solidarity and subsidiarity, according to which 'the rights of all individuals, families, and organizations and their practical implementation must be acknowledged'.[21] Finally, the question of *peace* must be mentioned. Certain pacifistic and ideological visions tend at times to secularize the value of peace, while, in other cases, there is the problem of summary ethical judgments which forget the complexity of the issues involved. Peace is always 'the work of justice and the effect of charity'.[22] It demands the absolute and radical rejection of violence and terrorism and requires a constant and vigilant commitment on the part of all political leaders.

*

---

21   Second Vatican Council, Pastoral Constitution *Gaudium et spes,* 75.
22   *Catechism of the Catholic Church,* No. 2304.

III. Principles of Catholic doctrine on the autonomy of the temporal order and on pluralism.

5. While a plurality of methodologies reflective of different sensibilities and cultures can be legitimate in approaching such questions, no Catholic can appeal to the principle of pluralism or to the autonomy of lay involvement in political life to support policies affecting the common good which compromise or undermine fundamental ethical requirements. This is not a question of 'confessional values' per se, because such ethical precepts are rooted in human nature itself and belong to the natural moral law. They do not require from those who defend them the profession of the Christian faith, although the Church's teaching confirms and defends them always and everywhere as part of her service to the truth about man and about the common good of civil society. Moreover, it cannot be denied that politics must refer to principles of absolute value precisely because these are at the service of the dignity of the human person and of true human progress.

6. The appeal often made to '*the rightful autonomy of the participation of lay Catholics*' in politics needs to be clarified. Promoting the common good of society,

according to one's conscience, has nothing to do with 'confessionalism' or religious intolerance. For Catholic moral doctrine, the rightful autonomy of the political or civil sphere from that of religion and the Church – *but not from that of morality* – is a value that has been attained and recognized by the Catholic Church and belongs to the inheritance of contemporary civilization.[23] John Paul II has warned many times of the dangers which follow from confusion between the religious and political spheres. 'Extremely sensitive situations arise when a specifically religious norm becomes or tends to become the law of a state without due consideration for the distinction between the domains proper to religion and to political society. In practice, the identification of religious law with civil law can stifle religious freedom, even going so far as to restrict or deny other inalienable human rights'.[24] All the faithful are well aware that specifically religious activities (such as the profession of faith, worship, administration of sacraments, theological doctrines, interchange between religious authorities and the members of religions) are outside the state's

---

23   Cf. Second Vatican Council, Pastoral Constitution *Gaudium et spes,* 76.
24   John Paul II, *Message for the 1991 World Day of Peace: 'If you want peace, respect the conscience of every person'*, 4: *AAS* 83 (1991), 414–415.

responsibility. The state must not interfere, nor in any way require or prohibit these activities, except when it is a question of public order. The recognition of civil and political rights, as well as the allocation of public services, may not be made dependent upon citizens' religious convictions or activities.

The right and duty of Catholics and all citizens to seek the truth with sincerity and to promote and defend, by legitimate means, moral truths concerning society, justice, freedom, respect for human life and the other rights of the person, is something quite different. The fact that some of these truths may also be taught by the Church does not lessen the political legitimacy or the rightful 'autonomy' of the contribution of those citizens who are committed to them, irrespective of the role that reasoned inquiry or confirmation by the Christian faith may have played in recognizing such truths. Such 'autonomy' refers first of all to the attitude of the person who respects the truths that derive from natural knowledge regarding man's life in society, even if such truths may also be taught by a specific religion, because truth is one. It would be a mistake to confuse the proper *autonomy* exercised by Catholics in political life with the claim of a principle that prescinds from the moral and social teaching of the Church.

By its interventions in this area, the Church's Magisterium does not wish to exercise political power or eliminate the freedom of opinion of Catholics regarding contingent questions. Instead, it intends – as is its proper function – to instruct and illuminate the consciences of the faithful, particularly those involved in political life, so that their actions may always serve the integral promotion of the human person and the common good. The social doctrine of the Church is not an intrusion into the government of individual countries. It is a question of the lay Catholic's duty to be morally coherent, found within one's conscience, which is one and indivisible. 'There cannot be two parallel lives in their existence: on the one hand, the so-called "spiritual life", with its values and demands; and on the other, the so-called "secular" life, that is, life in a family, at work, in social responsibilities, in the responsibilities of public life and in culture. The branch, engrafted to the vine which is Christ, bears its fruit in every sphere of existence and activity. In fact, every area of the lay faithful's lives, as different as they are, enters into the plan of God, who desires that these very areas be the "places in time" where the love of Christ is revealed and realized for both the glory of the Father and service of others. Every activity, every situation, every precise responsibility – as, for example, skill and solidarity in work, love and dedication in the family and the education of children, service to society and public life and the promotion of truth in the area of culture – are the occasions ordained by providence for a "continuous exercise" of faith, hope and charity' (*Apostolicam actuositatem*, 4)'.[25] Living and acting in conformity with one's own conscience on questions of politics is not slavish acceptance of positions alien to politics or some kind of confessionalism, but rather the way in which Christians offer their concrete contribution so that, through political life, society will become more just and more consistent with the dignity of the human person.

In democratic societies, all proposals are freely discussed and examined. Those who, on the basis of respect for individual conscience, would view the moral duty of Christians to act according to their conscience as something that disqualifies them from political life, denying the legitimacy of their political involvement following from their convictions about the common good, would be guilty of a form of intolerant *secularism*. Such a position would seek to deny not only any engagement of Christianity in public or political life, but even the possibility of natural ethics itself. Were this the case, the road would be open to moral anarchy, which would be anything but legitimate pluralism. The oppression of the weak

---

25   John Paul II, Apostolic Exhortation *Christifideles laici*, 59.

by the strong would be the obvious consequence. The marginalization of Christianity, moreover, would not bode well for the future of society or for consensus among peoples; indeed, it would threaten the very spiritual and cultural foundations of civilization.

IV. Considerations regarding particular aspects

7. In recent years, there have been cases within some organizations founded on Catholic principles, in which support has been given to political forces or movements with positions contrary to the moral and social teaching of the Church on fundamental ethical questions. Such activities, in contradiction to basic principles of Christian conscience, are not compatible with membership in organizations or associations which define themselves as Catholic. Similarly, some Catholic periodicals in certain countries have expressed perspectives on political choices that have been ambiguous or incorrect, by misinterpreting the idea of the political autonomy enjoyed by Catholics and by not taking into consideration the principles mentioned above.

Faith in Jesus Christ, who is 'the way, the truth, and the life' (Jn 14:6), calls Christians to exert a greater effort in building a culture which, inspired by the Gospel, will reclaim the values and contents of the Catholic

Tradition. The presentation of the fruits of the spiritual, intellectual and moral heritage of Catholicism in terms understandable to modern culture is a task of great urgency today, in order to avoid also a kind of Catholic cultural diaspora. Furthermore, the cultural achievements and mature experience of Catholics in political life in various countries, especially since the Second World War, do not permit any kind of 'inferiority complex' in comparison with political programs which recent history has revealed to be weak or totally ruinous. It is insufficient and reductive to think that the commitment of Catholics in society can be limited to a simple transformation of structures, because if at the basic level there is no culture capable of receiving, justifying and putting into practice positions deriving from faith and morals, the changes will always rest on a weak foundation.

Christian faith has never presumed to impose a rigid framework on social and political questions, conscious that the historical dimension requires men and women to live in imperfect situations, which are also susceptible to rapid change. For this reason, Christians must reject political positions and activities inspired by a utopian perspective which, turning the tradition of Biblical faith into a kind of prophetic vision without God, makes ill use of religion by directing consciences towards a hope which is merely earthly and which empties or reinterprets the Christian striving towards eternal life.

At the same time, the Church teaches that authentic freedom does not exist without the truth. 'Truth and freedom either go together hand in hand or together they perish in misery.'[26] In a society in which truth is neither mentioned nor sought, every form of authentic exercise of freedom will be weakened, opening the way to libertine and individualistic distortions and undermining the protection of the good of the human person and of the entire society.

8. In this regard, it is helpful to recall a truth which today is often not perceived or formulated correctly in public opinion: the right to freedom of conscience and, in a special way, to religious freedom, taught in the Declaration *Dignitatis humanae* of the Second Vatican Council, is based on the ontological dignity of the human person and not on a non-existent equality among religions or cultural systems of human creation.[27] Reflecting on this question, Paul

---

26   John Paul II, Encyclical Letter *Fides et ratio,* 90: *AAS* 91 (1999), 75.

27   Cf. Second Vatican Council, Declaration *Dignitatis humanae,* 1: 'This Sacred Council begins by professing that God himself has made known to the human race how men by serving him can be saved and reach the state of the blessed. We believe

VI taught that 'in no way does the Council base this right to religious freedom on the fact that all religions and all teachings, including those that are erroneous, would have more or less equal value; it is based rather on the dignity of the human person, which demands that he not be subjected to external limitations which tend to constrain the conscience in its search for the true religion or in adhering to it'.[28] The teaching on freedom of conscience and on religious freedom does not therefore contradict the condemnation of indifferentism and religious relativism by Catholic doctrine;[29] on the contrary, it is fully in accord with it.

---

that this one true religion subsists in the Catholic and Apostolic Church.' This does not lessen the sincere respect that the Church has for the various religious traditions, recognizing in them 'elements of truth and goodness'. See also, Second Vatican Council, Dogmatic Constitution *Lumen gentium,* 16; Decree *Ad gentes,* 11; Declaration *Nostra aetate,* 2; John Paul II, Encyclical Letter *Redemptoris missio,* 55: *AAS* 83 (1991), 302–304; Congregation for the Doctrine of the Faith, Declaration *Dominus Iesus,* 2, 8, 21: *AAS* 92 (2000), 742–765.

28   Paul VI, *Address to the Sacred College and to the Roman Prelature*: in *Insegnamenti di Paolo VI,* 14 (1976), 1088–1089.

29   Cf. Pius IX, Encyclical Letter *Quanta cura*: *ASS* 3 (1867), 162; Leo XIII, Encyclical Letter *Immortale Dei*: *ASS* 18 (1885), 170–171; Pius XI, Encyclical Letter *Quas primas*: *AAS* 17 (1925), 604–605; *Catechism of the Catholic Church,* No. 2108; Congregation for the Doctrine of the Faith, Declaration *Dominus Iesus,* 22.

V. Conclusion

9. The principles contained in the present *Note* are intended to shed light on one of the most important aspects of the unity of Christian life: coherence between faith and life, Gospel and culture, as recalled by the Second Vatican Council. The Council exhorted Christians 'to fulfil their duties faithfully in the spirit of the Gospel. It is a mistake to think that, because we have here no lasting city, but seek the city which is to come, we are entitled to shirk our earthly responsibilities; this is to forget that by our faith we are bound all the more to fulfil these responsibilities according to the vocation of each ... May Christians ... be proud of the opportunity to carry out their earthly activity in such a way as to integrate human, domestic, professional, scientific and technical enterprises with religious values, under whose supreme direction all things are ordered to the glory of God'.[30]

The Sovereign Pontiff John Paul II, in the Audience of 21 November 2002, approved the present Note,

---

30   Second Vatican Council, Pastoral Constitution *Gaudium et spes*, 43; see also John Paul II, Apostolic Exhortation *Christifideles laici*, 59.

adopted in the Plenary Session of this Congregation, and ordered its publication.[31]

Joseph Card. RATZINGER
Prefect
Tarcisio BERTONE, S.D.B.
Archbishop Emeritus of Vercelli Secretary

---

31 Cf. John Paul II, *Address to the Diplomatic Corps accredited to the Holy See*: *L'Osservatore Romano* (January 11, 2002).

Appendix 5

Considerations Regarding Proposals to Give Legal Recognition to Unions between Homosexual Persons

INTRODUCTION

1. In recent years, various questions relating to homosexuality have been addressed with some frequency by Pope John Paul II and by the relevant Dicasteries of the Holy See.[1] Homosexuality is a

---

1   Cf. John Paul II, *Angelus Messages* of 20 February 1994, and of 19 June, 1994; *Address to the Plenary Meeting of the Pontifical Council for the Family* (24 March 1999); *Catechism of the Catholic Church,* Nos. 2357–2359, 2396; Congregation for the Doctrine of the Faith, Declaration *Persona humana* (29 December 1975), 8; *Letter on the pastoral care of homosexual persons* (1 October, 1986); *Some considerations concerning the response to legislative proposals on the non-discrimination of homosexual persons* (24 July 1992); Pontifical Council for the Family, *Letter to the Presidents of the Bishops' Conferences of Europe on the resolution of the European Parliament regarding homosexual couples* (25 March 1994); *Family, marriage and 'de facto' unions* (26 July 2000), 23.

troubling moral and social phenomenon, even in those countries where it does not present significant legal issues. It gives rise to greater concern in those countries that have granted or intend to grant legal recognition to homosexual unions, which may include the possibility of adopting children. The present Considerations do not contain new doctrinal elements; they seek rather to reiterate the essential points on this question and provide arguments drawn from reason which could be used by Bishops in preparing more specific interventions, appropriate to the different situations throughout the world, aimed at protecting and promoting the dignity of marriage, the foundation of the family, and the stability of society, of which this institution is a constitutive element. The present Considerations are also intended to give direction to Catholic politicians by indicating the approaches to proposed legislation in this area which would be consistent with Christian conscience.[2] Since this question relates to the natural moral law, the arguments that follow are addressed not only to those who believe in Christ, but to all persons committed to promoting and defending the common good of society.

---

2   Cf. Congregation for the Doctrine of the Faith, *Doctrinal Note on some questions regarding the participation of Catholics in political life* (24 November 2002), 4.

I. The Nature of Marriage and Its Inalienable Characteristics

2. The Church's teaching on marriage and on the complementarity of the sexes reiterates a truth that is evident to right reason and recognized as such by all the major cultures of the world. Marriage is not just any relationship between human beings. It was established by the Creator with its own nature, essential properties and purpose.[3] No ideology can erase from the human spirit the certainty that marriage exists solely between a man and a woman, who by mutual personal gift, proper and exclusive to themselves, tend toward the communion of their persons. In this way, they mutually perfect each other, in order to cooperate with God in the procreation and upbringing of new human lives.

3. The natural truth about marriage was confirmed by the Revelation contained in the biblical accounts of creation, an expression also of the original human wisdom, in which the voice of nature itself is heard. There are three fundamental elements of the

---

3 Cf. Second Vatican Council, Pastoral Constitution *Gaudium et spes,* 48.

Creator's plan for marriage, as narrated in the Book of Genesis.

In the first place, man, the image of God, was created 'male and female' (Gen 1:27). Men and women are equal as persons and complementary as male and female. Sexuality is something that pertains to the physical–biological realm and has also been raised to a new level – the personal level – where nature and spirit are united.

Marriage is instituted by the Creator as a form of life in which a communion of persons is realized involving the use of the sexual faculty. 'That is why a man leaves his father and mother and clings to his wife and they become one flesh' (Gen 2:24).

Third, God has willed to give the union of man and woman a special participation in his work of creation. Thus, he blessed the man and the woman with the words 'Be fruitful and multiply' (Gen 1:28). Therefore, in the Creator's plan, sexual complementarity and fruitfulness belong to the very nature of marriage.

Furthermore, the marital union of man and woman has been elevated by Christ to the dignity of a sacrament. The Church teaches that Christian marriage is an efficacious sign of the covenant between Christ and the Church (cf. Eph 5:32). This Christian meaning of marriage, far from diminishing the profoundly human value of the marital union between man and woman, confirms and strengthens it (cf. Mt 19:3-12; Mk 10:6-9).

4. There are absolutely no grounds for considering homosexual unions to be in any way similar or even remotely analogous to God's plan for marriage and family. Marriage is holy, while homosexual acts go against the natural moral law. Homosexual acts 'close the sexual act to the gift of life. They do not proceed from a genuine affective and sexual complementarity. Under no circumstances can they be approved'.[4]

Sacred Scripture condemns homosexual acts 'as a serious depravity ... (cf. Rom 1:24-27; *1* Cor 6:10; *1* Tim 1:10). This judgment of Scripture does not of course permit us to conclude that all those who suffer from this anomaly are personally responsible for it, but it does attest to the fact that homosexual acts are intrinsically disordered'.[5] This same moral judgment is found in many Christian writers of the first centuries[6] and is unanimously accepted by Catholic Tradition.

---

4   *Catechism of the Catholic Church,* No. 2357.
5   Congregation for the Doctrine of the Faith, Declaration *Persona humana* (29 December 1975), 8.
6   Cf., for example, St. Polycarp, *Letter to the Philippians,* V, 3; St Justin Martyr, *First Apology,* 27, 1-4; Athenagoras, *Supplication for the Christians,* 34.

Nonetheless, according to the teaching of the Church, men and women with homosexual tendencies 'must be accepted with respect, compassion and sensitivity. Every sign of unjust discrimination in their regard should be avoided'.[7] They are called, like other Christians, to live the virtue of chastity.[8] The homosexual inclination is however 'objectively disordered'[9] and homosexual practices are 'sins gravely contrary to chastity'.[10]

II. Positions on the Problem of Homosexual Unions

5. Faced with the fact of homosexual unions, civil authorities adopt different positions. At times they simply tolerate the phenomenon; at other times they advocate legal recognition of such unions, under the pretext of avoiding, with regard to certain rights, discrimination against persons who live with someone of the same sex. In other cases, they favour giving homosexual unions legal equivalence

---

7   *Catechism of the Catholic Church,* No. 2358; cf. Congregation for the Doctrine of the Faith, *Letter on the pastoral care of homosexual persons* (1 October 1986), 10.

8   Cf. *Catechism of the Catholic Church,* No. 2359; cf. Congregation for the Doctrine of the Faith, *Letter on the pastoral care of homosexual persons* (1 October 1986), 12.

9   *Catechism of the Catholic Church,* No. 2358.

10   Ibid., No. 2396.

to marriage properly so-called, along with the legal possibility of adopting children.

Where the government's policy is *de facto* tolerance and there is no explicit legal recognition of homosexual unions, it is necessary to distinguish carefully the various aspects of the problem. Moral conscience requires that, in every occasion, Christians give witness to the whole moral truth, which is contradicted both by approval of homosexual acts and unjust discrimination against homosexual persons. Therefore, discreet and prudent actions can be effective; these might involve: unmasking the way in which such tolerance might be exploited or used in the service of ideology; stating clearly the immoral nature of these unions; reminding the government of the need to contain the phenomenon within certain limits so as to safeguard public morality and, above all, to avoid exposing young people to erroneous ideas about sexuality and marriage that would deprive them of their necessary defences and contribute to the spread of the phenomenon. Those who would move from tolerance to the legitimization of specific rights for cohabiting homosexual persons need to be reminded that the approval or legalization of evil is something far different from the toleration of evil.

In those situations where homosexual unions have been legally recognized or have been given the legal status and rights belonging to marriage, clear and emphatic opposition is a duty. One must refrain from any kind of formal cooperation in the enactment or application of such gravely unjust laws and, as far as possible, from material cooperation on the level of their application. In this area, everyone can exercise the right to conscientious objection.

III. Arguments from Reason Against Legal Recognition of Homosexual Unions

6. To understand why it is necessary to oppose legal recognition of homosexual unions, ethical considerations of different orders need to be taken into consideration.

From the order of right reason
The scope of the civil law is certainly more limited than that of the moral law,[11] but civil law cannot contradict right reason without losing its binding force on conscience.[12] Every humanly created law is legitimate insofar as it is consistent with the natural moral law, recognized by right reason, and insofar as

---

11 Cf. John Paul II, Encyclical Letter *Evangelium vitae* (25 March 1995), 71.
12 Cf. ibid., 72.

it respects the inalienable rights of every person.[13] Laws in favour of homosexual unions are contrary to right reason because they confer legal guarantees, analogous to those granted to marriage, to unions between persons of the same sex. Given the values at stake in this question, the State could not grant legal standing to such unions without failing in its duty to promote and defend marriage as an institution essential to the common good.

It might be asked how a law can be contrary to the common good if it does not impose any particular kind of behaviour, but simply gives legal recognition to a *de facto* reality which does not seem to cause injustice to anyone. In this area, one needs first to reflect on the difference between homosexual behaviour as a private phenomenon and the same behaviour as a relationship in society, foreseen and approved by the law, to the point where it becomes one of the institutions in the legal structure. This second phenomenon is not only more serious, but also assumes a more wide-reaching and profound influence, and would result in changes to the entire organization of society, contrary to the common good. Civil laws are structuring principles of man's life in society, for good or for ill. They 'play a very

---

13   Cf. St Thomas Aquinas, *Summa Theologiae,* I-II, q. 95, a. 2.

important and sometimes decisive role in influencing patterns of thought and behaviour'.[14] Lifestyles and the underlying presuppositions these express not only externally shape the life of society, but also tend to modify the younger generation's perception and evaluation of forms of behaviour. Legal recognition of homosexual unions would obscure certain basic moral values and cause a devaluation of the institution of marriage.

From the Biological and Anthropological Order

7. Homosexual unions are totally lacking in the biological and anthropological elements of marriage and family which would be the basis, on the level of reason, for granting them legal recognition. Such unions are not able to contribute in a proper way to the procreation and survival of the human race. The possibility of using recently discovered methods of artificial reproduction, beyond involving a grave lack of respect for human dignity,[15] does nothing to alter this inadequacy.

Homosexual unions are also totally lacking in the conjugal dimension, which represents the human and

---

14   John Paul II, Encyclical Letter *Evangelium vitae* (25 March 1995), 90.
15   Cf. Congregation for the Doctrine of the Faith, Instruction *Donum vitae* (22 February 1987), II. A. 1–3.

ordered form of sexuality. Sexual relations are human when and insofar as they express and promote the mutual assistance of the sexes in marriage and are open to the transmission of new life.

As experience has shown, the absence of sexual complementarity in these unions creates obstacles in the normal development of children who would be placed in the care of such persons. They would be deprived of the experience of either fatherhood or motherhood. Allowing children to be adopted by persons living in such unions would actually mean doing violence to these children, in the sense that their condition of dependency would be used to place them in an environment that is not conducive to their full human development. This is gravely immoral and in open contradiction to the principle, recognized also in the United Nations Convention on the Rights of the Child, that the best interests of the child, as the weaker and more vulnerable party, are to be the paramount consideration in every case.

From the social order

8. Society owes its continued survival to the family, founded on marriage. The inevitable consequence of legal recognition of homosexual unions would be the redefinition of marriage, which would become, in its legal status, an institution devoid of essential

reference to factors linked to heterosexuality; for example, procreation and raising children. If, from the legal standpoint, marriage between a man and a woman were to be considered just one possible form of marriage, the concept of marriage would undergo a radical transformation, with grave detriment to the common good. By putting homosexual unions on a legal plane analogous to that of marriage and the family, the State acts arbitrarily and in contradiction with its duties.

The principles of respect and non-discrimination cannot be invoked to support legal recognition of homosexual unions. Differentiating between persons or refusing social recognition or benefits is unacceptable only when it is contrary to justice.[16] The denial of the social and legal status of marriage to forms of cohabitation that are not and cannot be marital is not opposed to justice; on the contrary, justice requires it.

Nor can the principle of the proper autonomy of the individual be reasonably invoked. It is one thing to maintain that individual citizens may freely engage in those activities that interest them and that this falls within the common civil right to freedom; it is something quite different to hold that activities which

---

16   Cf. St Thomas Aquinas, *Summa Theologiae,* II-II, q. 63, a.1, c.

do not represent a significant or positive contribution to the development of the human person in society can receive specific and categorical legal recognition by the State. Not even in a remote analogous sense do homosexual unions fulfil the purpose for which marriage and family deserve specific categorical recognition. On the contrary, there are good reasons for holding that such unions are harmful to the proper development of human society, especially if their impact on society were to increase.

From the legal order

9. Because married couples ensure the succession of generations and are therefore eminently within the public interest, civil law grants them institutional recognition. Homosexual unions, on the other hand, do not need specific attention from the legal standpoint since they do not exercise this function for the common good.

Nor is the argument valid according to which legal recognition of homosexual unions is necessary to avoid situations in which cohabiting homosexual persons, simply because they live together, might be deprived of real recognition of their rights as persons and citizens. In reality, they can always make use of the provisions of law – like all citizens from the standpoint of their private autonomy – to protect their rights in matters of common interest. It would be gravely unjust to sacrifice the common good and just laws on the family in order to protect personal goods that can and must be guaranteed in ways that do not harm the body of society.[17]

IV. Positions of Catholic Politicians with Regard to Legislation in Favour of Homosexual Unions

10. If it is true that all Catholics are obliged to oppose the legal recognition of homosexual unions, Catholic politicians are obliged to do so in a particular way, in keeping with their responsibility as politicians. Faced with legislative proposals in favour of homosexual unions, Catholic politicians are to take account of the following ethical indications.

When legislation in favour of the recognition of homosexual unions is proposed for the first time in a legislative assembly, the Catholic law-maker has a moral duty to express his opposition clearly and

---

17   It should not be forgotten that there is always 'a danger that legislation which would make homosexuality a basis for entitlements could actually encourage a person with a homosexual orientation to declare his homosexuality or even to seek a partner in order to exploit the provisions of the law' (Congregation for the Doctrine of the Faith, *Some considerations concerning the response to legislative proposals on the non-discrimination of homosexual persons* [24 July 1992], 14).

publicly, and to vote against it. To vote in favour of a law so harmful to the common good is gravely immoral.

When legislation in favour of the recognition of homosexual unions is already in force, the Catholic politician must oppose it in the ways that are possible for him and make his opposition known; it is his duty to witness to the truth. If it is not possible to repeal such a law completely, the Catholic politician, recalling the indications contained in the Encyclical Letter *Evangelium vitae,* 'could licitly support proposals aimed at limiting the harm done by such a law and at lessening its negative consequences at the level of general opinion and public morality', on condition that his 'absolute personal opposition' to such laws was clear and well known and that the danger of scandal was avoided.[18] This does not mean that a more restrictive law in this area could be considered just or even acceptable; rather, it is a question of the legitimate and dutiful attempt to obtain at least the partial repeal of an unjust law when its total abrogation is not possible at the moment.

---

18   John Paul II, Encyclical Letter *Evangelium vitae* (25 March 1995), 73.

Conclusion

11. The Church teaches that respect for homosexual persons cannot lead in any way to approval of homosexual behaviour or to legal recognition of homosexual unions. The common good requires that laws recognize, promote and protect marriage as the basis of the family, the primary unit of society. Legal recognition of homosexual unions or placing them on the same level as marriage would mean not only the approval of deviant behaviour, with the consequence of making it a model in present-day society, but would also obscure basic values which belong to the common inheritance of humanity. The Church cannot fail to defend these values, for the good of men and women and for the good of society itself.

The Sovereign Pontiff John Paul II, in the Audience of 28 March 2003, approved the present Considerations, adopted in the Ordinary Session of this Congregation, and ordered their publication.

Joseph Card. RATZINGER
Prefect
Angelo Amato, S.D.B.
Titular Archbishop of Sila Secretary